D0837053

Level Up

Level Up
Copyright 2019, Joey Furjanic

Scripture quotations marked NASB are taken from the NEW AMERICAN STAN-
DARD BIBLE® (NASB), Copyright © 1960,1962,1963,1968,1971,1972,1973,1975,1
977,1995 by The Lockman Foundation. Used by permission. www.Lockman.org.

Scripture quotations marked NLT are taken from the Holy Bible, New Living Trans-
lation (NLT), Copyright © 1996, 2004, 2015 by Tyndale House Foundation. Used
by permission of Tyndale House Publishers, Inc., Carol Stream, IL 60188. All rights
reserved.

Scripture quotations marked (NIV) are taken from the Holy Bible, New International Version®, NIV®. Copyright © 1973, 1978, 1984, 2011 by Biblica, Inc.™ Used
by permission of Zondervan. All rights reserved worldwide. www.zondervan.com.
The "NIV" and "New International Version" are trademarks registered in the United
States Patent and Trademark Office by Biblica, Inc.™

Scripture quotations marked MSG are taken from *THE MESSAGE*, copyright ©
1993, 1994, 1995, 1996, 2000, 2001, 2002 by Eugene H. Peterson. Used by permission of NavPress. All rights reserved. Represented by Tyndale House Publishers,
Inc.

Scripture quotations marked ESV are from the ESV® Bible (The Holy Bible, English
Standard Version®), copyright © 2001 by Crossway, a publishing ministry of Good
News Publishers. Used by permission. All rights reserved.

Scripture quotations marked TPT are from The Passion Translation®. Copyright ©
2017, 2018 by Passion & Fire Ministries, Inc. Used by permission. All rights reserved. ThePassionTranslation.com.

Scripture quotations marked HCSB are taken from the Holman Christian Standard
Bible®, Copyright © 1999, 2000, 2002, 2003, 2009 by Holman Bible Publishers. Used
by permission. Holman Christian Standard Bible®, Holman CSB®, and HCSB® are
federally registered trademarks of Holman Bible Publishers.

Cover Design by **Anthony Gehin**

Interior Design by **Printopya**

Website: www.joeyfurjanic.org

ISBN: 978-1-949709-27-8

DEDICATION

To my wife, son, and parents. You are my teammates, my confidants, and my greatest blessings. Anything God does through me, I must attribute thanksgiving to your support, love, and leading. Enjoy.

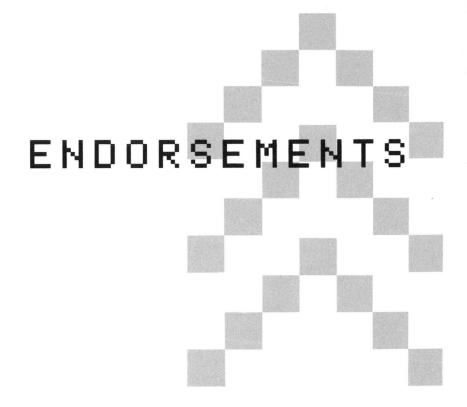

ENDORSEMENTS

"Relationships are the true currency of our life and legacy. In this book, my friend Pastor Joey Furjanic brings practical and real-life guidance on how to develop the relationships that matter most."

Chris Railey
Senior Director, Center for Leadership and Church
Development for the Assemblies of God

"To know Joey Furjanic is to know that his passions and convictions run deep. In *Level Up*, Joey challenges his generation to fight for healthy, God-honoring relationships in every area of life. If you're ready to live with purpose and integrity, then it's time to level up!"

Jenni Catron
Leadership coach and founder of The 4Sight Group

"I've been a fan of Pastor Joey Furjanic as a leader, pastor, and preacher for many years. Now, I have to add author and relationship expert to my fanboy list. Joey tackles every dimension of relationships with practical wisdom, humor, and biblical application. As a pastor and parent of four millennials, it is wisdom for them and me. I'll be buying multiple copies. 'Don't Waste Your Wait'—worth the price of the book. 'Integrity won't get you there fast, but it will get you there whole.' Yes and amen! Thanks, Joey, for a gift to your generation and mine."

Pastor Paul Taylor
Founding and Lead Pastor, Rivers Crossing
Community Church

"I have had the opportunity and privilege to be in close relationship with Pastor Joey Furjanic since he was in middle school. I am thoroughly impressed with his heart for people, passion for God, and giftedness as a leader! The reason I would strongly encourage you to read this book is that I know Joey has something valuable to say!"

Johnnie Wilson
Founder of Mainstream Orlando
Executive Pastor at Faith Assembly of God

"Our relationships largely define the trajectory of our lives. We need insightful, pastoral voices speaking God's truth into this topic today. In *Level Up*, Joey's pastoral heart is evident as he winsomely gives sound counsel and wisdom in navigating the complexities of our human interactions. His voice is a voice worth listening to, and this is a book you want to read."

Sam Deford
Pastor and artist, The Parks Church

"Joey Furjanic always brings something worth hearing to the conversation. He'll challenge and encourage you and help you take your relationships to the next level. Enjoy the read."

Kent Jacobs
Founding and Lead Pastor, Epic Church Philadelphia

"This is a remarkably well-written treatise on one of the foundational issues of life! Joey Furjanic cites statistics such as 'The number of Americans with no close friends has tripled since 1985!' But then he gives us hope—hope for ourselves, our dates, our marriages, our friends, and our future. This intriguing, revealing, insightful work was meant for millennials, but I felt it speaking to me as a Baby Boomer as well. I highly recommend it."

JD Pearring
Director of Excel Leadership Network

"Joey's refreshing approach to the subject of relationships is real and authentic. His voice is one of candor and transparency and reaches deep into the core of how humanity is wired to be connected with others. *Level Up* beautifully highlights the power and importance of intentionally seeking health and wholeness in relational connections."

Josh Alltop
Consultant and Dove Award-winning producer

"Do you need to better yourself? Your life? Your relationships? Then you need to level up! Pastor Joey delivers an inspiring and life-changing revelation on how to be a better you, to be a better friend, and to have better relationships."

Moises Santana
International Evangelist

"Joey Furjanic is a powerful, fresh voice to a generation that is full of untapped potential. He communicates with insight, humor, and passion. Level Up will inspire you to step up and rise higher in the most strategic relationships God has given you. If you want to maximize your relational influence, then this is the book for you."

Brad Leach
Founder and Lead Pastor, City Life Philly

TABLE OF CONTENTS

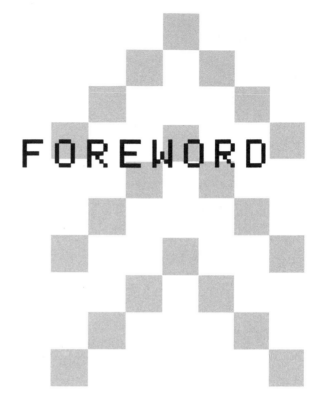

FOREWORD

Relationships are currency in the kingdom. We live in a society that exalts terms like "self-made" and perpetuates the idea that the ultimate goal in life is to achieve independence. The kingdom of God operates differently. In the kingdom, independence is immaturity. The kingdom operates by interdependence, a shared need for God and one another. The apostle Paul writes it this way: "But our bodies have many parts, and God has put each part just where he wants it. How strange a body would be if it had only one part! Yes, there are many parts, but only one body. The eye can never say to the hand, 'I don't need you.' The head can't say to the feet, 'I don't need you'" (1 Corinthians 12:18-21, NLT).

The topic of relationships is one of the most important in all of life because in order to have a successful life we must have meaningful relationships. My good friend pastor Joey Furjanic has been a successful relationship builder his entire life. The depth and diversity of those around him serve as an example of his understanding of people and relational dynamics. In a tribal and segmented society, we need now more than ever to understand how to not just survive but also to thrive in this area. In this new book, *Level Up*, my friend not only tackles the interpersonal dynamic of relationship but also the internal dynamic.

Scripture records an important interaction between Jesus and the religious leaders of the day that reveals one of the most important keys of relationship:

> But when the Pharisees heard that he had silenced the Sadducees with his reply, they met together to question him again. One of them, an expert in religious law, tried to trap him with this question: "Teacher, which is the most important commandment in the law of Moses?" Jesus replied, "'You must love the LORD your God with all your heart, all your soul, and all your mind.' This is the first and greatest commandment. A second is equally important: 'Love your neighbor as yourself.' The entire law and all the demands of the prophets are based on these two commandments." (Matthew 22:34-40, NLT)

The apostle Paul picks up on the same statement: "For the whole law can be summed up in this one command: 'Love your neighbor as yourself'" (Galatians 5:14, NLT).

This shows us that internal and interpersonal relationship mastery are connected. You cannot love others if you don't love yourself. Conversely, you are to love others as you love yourself.

If the law of human nature is self-preservation (selfishness), then it is necessary that we learn Christ's nature, which is self-lessness.

I'm so glad Joey has written this book. We need it in this culture. Having moved to Philadelphia and planted a multicultural, multiethnic, multigenerational church in the midst of a segmented and tribal time, his voice is invaluable. He and his wife, Lauren, are two of the most loving and authentic people you will ever meet. They will walk through fire and back with people because they genuinely love people from their core. Their life experiences qualify them to speak to all aspects of relationships—from self to romance to friendships to the relational dynamics within institutions. The church, which I'm particularly passionate about, has uniquely been authorized by God to model for the world the ultimate goal of healthy relationships, which is unity. How we see the church and relate to and within the church impacts how the world sees the church and, ultimately, Christ.

As you read you'll be impacted by the authenticity and passion that ooze from Joey every time you hear him speak, not only publicly but privately too.

Joey is a friend I love and cherish, and after you read you'll easily see why. Allow the pages of this book to take you to the next level of relationship. It's time to level up!

William McDowell
Lead pastor of Deeper Fellowship Church in Orlando, Florida; world-renowned worship leader; Grammy Award nominee; and author of *It's Happening*

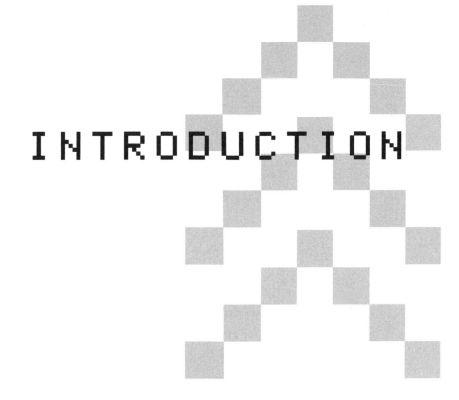

INTRODUCTION

The framework of this book is crafted in hopes that we might experience deeper maturity and higher growth regarding ourselves, interpersonal relationships, romance, and authority. More specifically, I wrote this book with my generation, the Millennials, in mind. If we're honest, the culture we navigate through doesn't always lend itself to quality community. Why? Because it is so easy (and sometimes celebrated) to hide, ghost, and avoid confrontation. I happen to think we're better than that, and I believe we can all agree that healthy relationships can make our disunified world a better place. That's why I decided to write this book and call it *Level Up*, a phrase that embodies the action of working toward greater things. I want to reach a higher level, to shape our world into something better. In order to do this, we must recognize that unity, authenticity, and a better world begin with you and me. It begins with us taking our own baggage seriously and allowing the timeless principles of God's Word to embody our thinking, moving, and being. That's the goal of this book: to get you to "level up" in your relationships and, in turn, experience your own personal victory while partnering with God in bringing true hope to every person you come in contact with.

START WITH ME

Family history is incredibly important to the makeup of who we are and eventually what we become. Many of the friends and family I grew up around experienced divorce, financial uncertainty, instability in their living situation, and domestic abuse. I'm sure I've already touched a nerve and covered a large percentage of my readers with that last sentence. The truth is, if you've grown up over the last fifty years, statistics show that 40 percent of us or more have experienced some sort of broken or incomplete home scenario.[1]

I live just a few blocks away from one of the largest open-air drug markets in the US. I've walked the streets and have seen firsthand the devastation of this crisis, not only on the streets of Kensington but in my own family as well. From suicides, deaths too soon, addiction, and unexpected disappointments, I'm sure many of you have experienced the same thing with some of your loved ones. Additionally, the church I pastor supports a recovery house that sits in the middle of the "drug war zone." From know-

1. Glenn Allen and Jadine S. Jett, "Stats of Effects in Broken Homes," *Richmond Times-Dispatch*, January 30, 2013.

ing the addicted and hearing their stories, we find that great pain and disappointment experienced throughout their formative years are prevalent themes that drive many (not all) to addiction. For most, what started as a momentary way out of reality turned into a deeper pit of real-life slavery. So whether we like to admit it or not, how we grew up and what was accepted or ignored in our home affect how we interact with others and how we view ourselves. These realities can manifest later in life and lead to dark places, such as addiction, prison, broken relationships, horrible anxieties, or even suicide.

Because my parents loved me and stayed together, I experienced an acceleration of confidence and success in my life, for which I'm grateful. However, I also know that even in a "together" home, there can be broken pasts, incorrect patterns, and unhealed hearts. When I look at my family history, I see major gaps of health. Like many of us, there is major addiction and abuse woven throughout the fabric of my family history. There's also murder, mental illness, shame, divorce, and disappointment. Great fear and anxiety exist in my family, too, and may in yours as well. I, you, we, could go on and on, but I'll spare you.

That being said, you know what else is in my family history? Hard work. Loyalty. A mustard seed of faith. Passion. Forgiveness. Adventure. A pioneering spirit. Risk. Patriotism. Overachieving. An underdog spirit. I'm proud of these traits and carry them intrinsically. We all have good and bad family tendencies that have been passed down to us. Interestingly, some of the very things we hate about our family or ourselves have the potential to propel us to higher realms of success when we learn to manage them correctly. Crazy to think, right?

What am I saying? Well, I need you to understand that *winning in relationships has so much to do with understanding yourself and experiencing victory over your own demons.* The reality is, we all have challenges that have been passed down to us, and unfortunately, we have probably grabbed some unnecessary baggage along the way as well. Maybe some of those lingering mistakes have affected current and past relationships in your life. Take a breath and remember that all relationships are *work*, and often the most fruitful and healthy relationships develop when *we*, you and I, put in the personal work to know ourselves and rest on the spiritual surgical table. You may be thinking, *Maybe the ship has sailed and certain relationships are unlikely to be restored.* That's hard. I get it.

Still, there's hope for today and tomorrow. I'm a believer in the power of redemption and the magnificent work of grace. God did miracles then and can still do them today. There's even hope to make peace with relationships in which someone has passed on from this life. That's *hope*. And this is a book about hope. This is a book about victory. This is a book about enjoying your journey with yourself and others, not just enduring your numbered days. You're going to smile again. Laugh again. Run again. You're going to win again *or* be victorious for the very first time. That's good news; that's hope!

As you read, my prayer is not only that you apply these practical principles but also that you continually take personal inventory of your own health. I hope you will become more self-aware, vulnerable, and honest than you ever have before. As you put the personal work in, you can experience the most beautiful part of life, which is peace with yourself, fluidity with others, and vibrancy with God. While this book isn't necessarily about marriage, business, parenting, money, or entrepreneurship, I believe many of these principles will serve you well in every area of your life—especially because life, in most ways, is about relationships. Ready to level up? Let's go.

PART 1

ME, MYSELF,
AND I

CHAPTER 1

KNOW THYSELF

"Know your enemy and know yourself and you can fight a hundred battles without disaster."
-Sun Tzu

When I was in high school, football was the centerpiece of my existence. I started playing varsity at the end of my freshman year and never looked back. My favorite pro team, the Philadelphia Eagles, went to four straight conference championships during that time as well. My weekend consisted of high school football on Friday nights and watching college football on Saturdays in preparation for the "Birds" game on Sunday. My mom would take us to the early church service so that we could make it back in time for the 1 pm kick-off. We'd stop at the bagel shop next to the sports bar to grab tuna, cream cheese, everything bagels, and soda. She would cut tomatoes and red onions to place on the bagels and would serve these with fried potatoes. I still love tomato and red onion today on anything—potatoes too, but that's to my detriment. Because we lived in Orlando, Florida, the Eagles rarely played on the regular channels, and there was no NFL Sunday Ticket, so we had to get home and eat our bagels quickly, watch the pregame show, and hustle over to the sports bar to watch the game. Even then we'd end up getting stuck with the Buccaneers, Jaguars, or Dolphins—

yuck! Those Sundays were fun and formative times, and it was a great opportunity for my father and me to bond as well.

As I write this, I can't help but think of my son, Maverick, who was born on September 1, 2017, just in time for the Eagles' first Super Bowl winning season. Holding my son in the center of Philadelphia, at the church we started, as we won the Super Bowl was absolutely priceless. Heaven on Earth is the best way to describe it. I wish my dad could have stood there with us, but I could hear him in my heart saying, "Can you believe it?" over and over, and me replying out loud, "*No*, they're lying to us!"

Stay with me; I'm going somewhere with this. The purpose of these stories is to help you understand my personality and tendencies, and hopefully you'll be able to identify some of your own as I share mine.

My football team was bad in high school. We lost almost every Friday, and when I would get home, I'd gripe and head to my room. I would barely come out until I had to Sunday morning. I was so frustrated, angry, embarrassed, and disappointed by losing that it would pin me to my bed and consume me. I remember one year on my birthday weekend, the Eagles lost the conference championship (the game before the Super Bowl) *again*. I was so irritated that I took all of my posters, pictures, jerseys, and autographs and put them in a box in the fireplace. First of all, why did we have a fireplace in Florida? Second, I'm glad my mom wouldn't let me burn it, because I know I would have.

I took perfection so seriously that I couldn't see straight. Why? Was it insecurity? Fear? Pride? Certainly, an ounce of parental or godly fear is healthy, and so is a bit of pride. I'm not talking about arrogance, but the ability to hold your head high and walk confidently in your work or experience joy over your team winning. Having a competitive nature is not wrong either. However, my emotions were unhealthy and stemmed from somewhere deeper. *I served my emotions rather than my emotions serving me.* In fact, it's something I still struggle with today, and, I imagine, you may too.

Later on in life, as I started to preach and counsel, I began to understand some of my own issues more clearly as they would come out as advice I didn't know was in me. For instance, I love my mother very much. Besides my wife, she is my best friend and biggest cheerleader. I'm also aware that she had a very challenging childhood and things happened to her that I wouldn't wish on anyone.

There is a huge age gap between my parents. My mom grew up during the sexual revolution decades, where drugs were normal and partners were vast. This comes with its own baggage. My dad, on the other hand, grew up in America's "Greatest Generation." He is a WWII product, served in the Navy, and even had a wife and family before he met my mother. My dad was raised in a time in which you didn't complain, you made it work, you innovated, and you did what you had to for your country and family. I'm not sure the phrases "I love you," "I'm proud of you," or "you can do whatever you dream" were a part of his equation. Because of this, I'm aware that my Eastern European heritage comes with a tenacity and grit that don't always lend themselves to sensitivity. Of course, when your childhood is built on survival or neglect, this affects your path in life. Without the key ingredient of a healthy home and regular, loving communication, our confidence is limited and our self-image can get skewed.

As I mentioned in the introduction, even in my together home, I was experiencing fragments of my parents' incompletions. Going back even further, both sets of my grandparents had significant challenges of their own. My mom's mom, for instance, was abused and tossed around between different homes and boarding schools. She also had miscarriages, six kids, lost her only son, and overcame alcoholism through it all. My mom's dad served in the Army, had an incomplete relationship with his father, and married my grandmother at sixteen years old. Sixteen and married? Wow. Recognizing my own immaturities (and not speaking for others), I cannot even imagine getting married that young.

The point I'm making is that my parents were fragile, incomplete, and unhealthy, even after they became Christians. For clarity, becoming a Christian does not immediately eliminate our issues; by God's grace, it illuminates our issues and mercifully leads us toward the fresh waters of freedom. I love that about God, and I love that about following Jesus. He leads us by still waters and takes His time in both revealing our problems and healing our brokenness. Sadly, for many of us it becomes too painful to deal with, so we run *from* instead of running *to*, leaving our relationships and souls to pay the price.

Early on in my life, my parents took a big risk and moved from Philadelphia to Orlando to start a new branch of their company. God is so sovereign, and I'm convinced this move saved our lives. I do not think I would be alive today had my parents not left Philadelphia. How do I know? Considering all of the groundwork I laid about my family history, I'm confident I would have been a disaster, and due to the stark similarities between my mother and me, we would have killed each other (not an exaggeration).

Through years of deep work in my soul, I can pinpoint the reason I was so intense about losing and why I took it (and sometimes still take it) so personally. Simple answer: *fear*. It runs deep in my family. It is a root and stronghold that has taken residence over generations, and growing up, we didn't know how to fight it. So, when things looked like they were out of our hands (i.e., losing), we'd cling to control because that daunting spirit of fear would rear its nasty head, and clinging to frustration was a chemical release that carried us toward a form of stability and control.

What was I afraid of, you ask? Losing my position on the field, being replaced, what others thought of me, not having an opportunity again, letting others down, letting myself down, not getting a scholarship, never accomplishing anything with my life, having an insignificant existence, etc. Most of these things were incredibly irrational, but my fear resulted in angry outbursts, anxiety, extreme negativity, and fights. *These were all symptoms of a fear problem that I allowed to take root in me, and without being aware of these tendencies, my best future was at risk.* Unless we are aware of and working on these harmful traits, our best lives could be hindered.

So, what does any of this have to do with relationships? To be completely honest, I still struggle with fear quite a bit. Heck, I'm even afraid to fly in a plane and I have to fly all the time. This is ridiculous because there is a one-in-eleven-million chance that I will die in a plane crash, yet I have an irrational fear of flying.[2] If I

2. Ben Bowman, "How Do People Survive Plane Crashes?" Curiosity.com. August 2, 2017.

let fear win, I wouldn't be able to expand our ministry, go to necessary conferences, take my family on vacation, or see the world. Fortunately, I've been to almost twenty different countries and have been on ministry trips to Europe eight different times. How? Because *I refuse to allow fear to rob me of all God has for me.* Yet there have been plenty of times I've allowed fear to win and have lost my temper over things both rational and irrational.

This, of course, affects every relationship in my life. Because of fear, I can say things I don't mean or shouldn't say. Because of fear, I hold back from stepping out and doing something I need to, simply because I can't control the outcome. Because of fear, I can be too stern with an employee or take my stresses out on my wife or my parents. Thankfully, I have the scriptures to teach me, friends to encourage me, a staff to remind me, and a family who loves me enough to help me identify the insufficiencies in myself that do not belong. You need that too, which is why it is so important to know yourself.

COMBATTING YOUR DEMONS

In 2 Samuel 11, King David gives in to a moment of weakness and all hell breaks loose:

One evening David got up from his bed and walked around on the roof of the palace. From the roof he saw a woman bathing. The woman was very beautiful, and David sent someone to find out about her. The man said, "She is Bathsheba, the daughter of Eliam and the wife of Uriah the Hittite." (2 Samuel 11:2-3, NLT)

This moment in history triggers a series of unnecessary tragedies and trials that never had to happen. David goes on to have an affair with Bathsheba, gets her pregnant, kills Bathsheba's husband as a cover-up for her newfound pregnancy, eventually loses the baby, and begins a generational curse of lust, bloodshed, and disloyalty. As a result, David cannot build the temple of the Lord he wishes to build due to the amount of bloodshed on his hands. David's son Amnon goes on to rape his own sister. David's son Absalom (whom he loved deeply) kills Amnon and leads a rebellion against David to usurp his throne. David's rebellion against a godly prophet leads to a plague that infects his people. David's son Solomon (though remarkably wise) concludes his life on the brink of depression and misery, though he had more riches, wives, and sexual partners than anyone in the history of the world. What a mess! Sin is a nasty disease that spreads like wildfire throughout our relationships and families. This is why we must be vigilant in knowing ourselves and continue being aware of our unhealthy propensities.

Paul says, "I don't really understand myself, for I want to do what is right, but I don't do it. Instead, I do what I hate" (Romans 7:15, NLT).

I feel like that sometimes, and I bet you do too. In the next few verses of Romans 7, Paul goes on to say that he wants to do the right thing but can't because of his unwanted marriage with sin. He closes with thanksgiving and claims that there is hope for freedom because of Jesus. I echo the same sentiment. We really do have a hope for freedom and restoration in and because of Jesus. How? Well, He is an ever-present help in time of need. Since His Spirit lives within us, our ability to understand ourselves and have victory over our unwanted tendencies is greatly available.

Go with me a bit further: "The human heart is the most deceitful of all things, and desperately wicked. Who really knows how bad it is?" (Jeremiah 17:9, NLT).

Have you ever heard the phrase "trust your heart"? Don't you dare! That's a bad move, unless your heart has been transformed and regenerated. In Ephesians 4, the apostle Paul goes on to share that when we are in Christ, we are transformed and given a new mind, a new heart, and a new purpose. Jesus Himself teaches that when we ask for help, He sends us the "advocate" (His Spirit) to abide in us and illuminate all areas of sin, need, and purpose. Without the invitation and activity of the Spirit in our lives, we are most susceptible to naturally destructive tendencies. *But*, when we actively pursue personal wholeness, spiritual renewal, emotional health, and identifying unhealthy family traits, we experience the benefit in several ways:

1. Our peace and confidence greatly increase.
2. Our work and dreams experience more clarity and momentum.
3. Our interpersonal relationships (family, friends, romantic relationships) become more fulfilling and healthy.
4. Our journey with God enhances and produces lasting fruit.

As I close this chapter, I want to reiterate why I chose to open the book with this content. Your personal awareness and emotional health are the keys that unlock the deepest fulfillment in your life and will stimulate the best part of living, which is true covenant relationships with others. So ask yourself, "What is it I need to be healthy? Is it a break from dating? Is it counseling? Is it a regular rhythm of exercise and eating better? Is it understanding my family deeper?" I cannot answer these for you, but as you seek help, you will know the right steps to take, and I strongly encourage you to take them. *You will never regret investing into your soul; it pays out like no other investment can.*

CHAPTER 2

SINGLE, SEXY, AND SATISFIED

"Power is sexy, not simply in its own right, but because it inspires self-confidence in its owner and a shiver of subservience on the part of those who approach it."
-Barbara Amiel

I got married at the ripe age of twenty-six years old. I am quite confident that I didn't get married a day too soon or a day too late. It was the right time *for me*. "For me" is a phrase we should embrace a little more, and I don't mean that in a self-consumed, narcissistic sort of way. I mean it in a "I know myself and I'm not ready" or "I'm good right now; it can wait" sort of way. Make sense? We live in an age of constant comparison. At our fingertips, we see the world through a screen and fantasize about all the things we're missing out on in the current moment. We see everyone's highlights and die a little inside because someone is further along in life or "happier" than we are, from what we can see. I believe social media is this generation's greatest curse and greatest blessing wrapped in one. Carey Nieuwhof once said, "Social media makes for a great servant but a terrible master."[3] Ain't that the truth! It takes us further than we could dream but can cut us deeper than we wish.

While the majority of us know this to be true, it's still hard to manage the tensions we face in the world around us. Even as a pastor, I struggle with comparison and give way to unnecessary anxieties. I find myself asking the questions "How does this pastor have so many people and resources?" or "How did 46,000 people get 'saved' in one service?" *Comparison breeds contempt and leads me to follow someone else's calling instead of my own.* You've been there, I'm sure of it. What's that have to do with being *single, sexy, and satisfied*? Everything!

The reality is, comparison steals our confidence; and confidence can be a vehicle that takes us from success to success, an engine that gives flight to many dreams and innovations, and it can serve as a lightning rod of attraction. You've heard it said before, but sexiness isn't found in shape, size, look, or feel, but in confidence. So, why are we so busy comparing and complaining when we could be working on our confidence? In this chapter, I want to teach you how to vibe again, acquire confidence, enjoy being single, and love the gift of the relationship status you've been given. I can confidently declare that being single is a blessing that is very much worth embracing.

---

3. Craig Goeschel, "Struggles—Rest," *About Church Online, Life.Church*, October 6, 2014. www.life.church/media/struggles/rest/.

SINGLE

First of all, being single is a gift. Don't get it twisted. Marriage is not the "promised land" and neither is moving in with your partner and acting like you're married. Your promised land is connected to your purpose and your mission. Whether you're single, engaged, married, married with kids, an empty nester, or a widow(er), you need to know that no other human being can fully satisfy or complete you. If you confuse that, either everyone in your life will disappoint you or your spouse, boyfriend/girlfriend, or children will become an idol that will distance you from God and keep you from developing necessary emotional health.

There are several outstanding single ladies in the church I pastor, as I'm sure is the case in churches all around the world. In fact, one of my location pastors is a truly remarkable single woman. I often have conversations with her and other ladies about what their singleness means to them. These talks can be challenging yet fun and usually lead to us joking about how they wish the guys in our church would "level up." As we converse about singleness, many times we refer to 1 Corinthians, where Paul, one of the best known writers in the Bible, talks about his own singleness. He even goes so far as to say that he wishes everyone he was writing to were single just like him! What? That's crazy! Not exactly. Paul makes some pretty good points:

But I wish everyone were single, just as I am. . . . I want you to be free from the concerns of this life. An unmarried man can spend his time doing the Lord's work and thinking how to please him. But a married man has to think about his earthly responsibilities and how to please his wife. His interests are divided. In the same way, a woman who is no longer married or has never been married can be devoted to the Lord and holy in body and in spirit. But a married woman has to think about her earthly responsibilities and how to please her husband. I am saying this for your benefit, not to place restrictions on you. I want you to do whatever will help you serve the Lord best, with as few distractions as possible. (1 Corinthians 7:7,32-35, NLT)

As a married man, I can tell you that Paul is *preaching*! I love being married and I wouldn't trade it for anything. Still, there were elements of being single that were simply easier and cheaper. Then I had a child and life got even more complicated. Don't get me wrong; I love being a father and wouldn't trade it for anything. I also wouldn't wish my responsibilities on anyone who isn't ready or called to manage it. Now, I'm not so naive as to think that a single person in my church or one of my Instagram followers isn't, at times, plagued with concern about their future when I post adorable pictures of my son or date nights with my wife. John Ortberg says in his blog, "The yearning to attach and connect, to love and be loved, is the fiercest longing of the soul." The legitimacy of desiring partnership and family is real, it's healthy, and it's more than okay. However, where a single person can be wrong is in thinking that these elements alone bring fulfillment. They simply do not. They aren't meant to.

Singleness is a godly experience, carved out for those He trusts and is preparing. Unfortunately, in the American church particularly, *we've highlighted marriage as the peak of the mountain, when marriage really is a fresh start at the bottom of the hill.* I don't mean that negatively at all, as marriage has extraordinary views. Nevertheless, everyone needs to know that a good marriage is more work than a hundred ants constructing a pyramid. Being single has a significant place in the climb, too, and just because you have to take a selfie by yourself doesn't make the picture any less beautiful. If we devalue singles in the church, we are deeply hurting some of the most valuable congregants and ministers we have. We are also not creating a space for those who have chosen celibacy, are confused about and working out their sexuality, or who desire vocational ministry or church leadership but aren't currently married.

It is a serious offense to throw out and devalue the single, just as it is a serious offense for the single to waste their season of singleness with complaining. Sadly, some stay single when they don't have to be, because they've refused to graduate the course of preparation God is taking them on. *Every season of your life is a seed.* You must ask yourself, "What seeds am I sowing today?" because you will reap something significant tomorrow, good or bad. If you're single, embrace it. There's something fruitful for you right where you are. And remember, when you get to eternity, God is not going to ask you how many kids you had or if you had great sex. Not that He doesn't care about those things, but He's going to be interested in our faithfulness. *Therefore, don't be unfaithful just because you're unmarried.*

SEXY

That's a racy subtitle for a chapter in a Christian book, Pastor Joey, isn't it? Yeah, I know. Relax. Another word for sexy is "swag."

We all need our own form of swag, and I don't mean a "swag bag" (Stuff We All Get). Here's what I mean: it is healthy to have or do things that help make up our persona and leverage a greater purpose in our life—for instance, a job or career, a hobby or interest, or a particular passion or endeavor we're pursuing. In addition to our relationship with God, or because of our relationship with God, *what we do helps attract what we need.*

A quality romantic relationship or good friendships are great additions to your current life. These people will (or should) complement you and serve as much-needed teammates in your life's journey. The best way to attract the people you need is to have something in your life that is attractive. Imagine yourself with a job, a savings account, a dream, stories to tell, your own place, your own vehicle, or clarity on your purpose in life. How much more attractive would you be to others?

Now, I'm not suggesting we pursue these things just to please other people or to garner attention. I'm not suggesting you need to be a millionaire or own your own house either. What I'm saying is that when you have some swag, it is naturally going to draw people toward you. *I also believe that when you have your own things happening, it can serve as a protecting agent from getting dangerously attached or too dependent on other relationships.*

HERE'S HOW TO KNOW YOU NEED YOUR OWN SWAG

- You've stopped hanging with your good friends and family.
- You've lost your passion and forgotten your dreams.
- You're bored.
- You're broke.

- You won't do anything alone.
- You aren't happy unless you're attached to a specific person.
- You have major anxiety about your singleness.
- Your self-confidence is low.

I've heard and witnessed countless scenarios in which some-body has lost or gained their confidence. Here are some practical things to do to acquire the natural swag that you need:

Save some money: You'd be surprised how confident you would feel if you applied some financial discipline for several months; and the next thing you know, you've got thousands of dollars in your savings account. Talk about being able to breathe and having options!

Turn off your phone: I dare you to practice taking time away from your phone or social media every once in a while. The endor-phins you've trained to reward your brain for getting a like, com-ment, post, or share will hate you and thank you at the same time.

See a counselor: There is no doubt that communicating what's going on or what's happened in your life could set you free and provide much-needed healing, resulting in a new wave of confi-dence and peace. If you can't afford a counselor, start by reading *Emotionally Healthy Spirituality* by Peter Scazzero.

Try something new: Often, when we attempt something we're afraid of and succeed at it, this produces a new level of confidence to try again at something we've failed at in the past or are afraid of in the present.

Make a change: Whether it's drastic or subtle, change something. It could be a diet, fashion style, a daily life rhythm that contributes to unhealthy patterns, an old habit, or overdone tradition—*break it!* When we make a change and get out of a rut, it opens our eyes to new possibilities and perspectives.

Now go ahead, level up and get your swag back!

SATISFIED

This portion of the chapter is essential to your personal development and lends you qualifying features that will most certainly add value to others. Go with me and allow me to teach you, from God's Word, to be truly satisfied.

I love the saying "Happiness isn't about getting what you want but wanting what you have." Many people have said it a million different ways, but Paul started the quote when he said,

> I know what it is to be in need, and I know what it is to have plenty. I have learned the secret of being content in any and every situation, whether well fed or hungry, whether living in plenty or in want. I can do all this through him [Christ] who gives me strength. (Philippians 4:12-13, NIV)

Remember, many theologians suggest that Paul is writing this letter from initial custody (waiting for sentencing), or even prison. He's basically telling people on the outside how to be free, content, and satisfied, while he's locked up with no way out. Where does this grit and determination come from? I want this. It's truly remarkable, and I believe that, no matter your situation, you can live with that kind of vigor, joy, peace, and gladness.

I have a dear friend who is quite a bit older than I am, quite brilliant, and lived an adventurous life before she landed at our church in Philly. She has read more books than days I've lived, and she's also one of the best cooks I've ever met. Even my wife loves her food, which says something, because Lauren doesn't eat anyone's food except her mother's and her own. Anyway, this woman is one of my confidants, my biggest blessings thus far, and my greatest encouragers. She doesn't mess around, always tells me the truth (even when I don't ask for it), and calls me out on anything that reeks of inauthenticity. I love that about her, and I need this voice in my life. She's also a really tough nut to crack, and when you hear her story, you'll understand why.

Growing up in a family of nine, connecting with Mom and Dad was extremely difficult. Especially because Dad was a womanizer, abuser, and a drunk. Mom was disengaged, uninterested in love, and emotionally distant. In an environment like this, emotional and physical abuse were frequent, and forming healthy relationships became challenging as well. While the home was a mess on the inside and full of mental illness, to the rest of the world this was a happy, wealthy, and important family. Dad was very popular in the community, and the family was extraordinarily well-educated and connected. *Isn't it amazing that you can have it all and have nothing at the same time?*

As childhood ended and college approached, my friend was introduced to Jesus through a campus ministry. However, experiencing the grace and mercy that a relationship with Jesus had to offer was challenging for my friend because of her broken and painful upbringing. She leaned much more on the rigid rules of a religious Christianity, understanding the letter of the law without the spirit of it. Even still, she started heading in a direction of hope, crediting this college ministry for ultimately saving her life.

Around this time, my friend met a "Christian" man right after college and married him quickly. Sadly, this man was confused, mentally ill, and more broken than I have time to expound on. Divorce ensued after a short five years. Thus began her journey of travel, new jobs, deeper education, and therapy, all the while living life an arm's length away from relational intimacy. Through the years, more reminders of her painful childhood surfaced as brothers became addicts, resulting in job losses and deaths; her sisters dealt with emotional scars; and her parents passed on from this life. From coast to coast, job to job, friend to friend, and church to church, this doctor had major choices to make about the rest of her days. I believe she has made the right ones.

I don't know if I've ever met someone with more tenacity and passion, who is as honest, vulnerable, and clear minded as my friend. She is one of the most generous people I know and would open her home to a stranger, talk to the lonely, care for the crazy, and adventure to the ends of the earth. Now full of laughter, tears, wisdom, and opinions, I know there are still lingering effects of past damage. I also know there has been extraordinary healing, deep joy, and true satisfaction. As a single woman, knowing that marriage or having her own family may not be an option at this point, she has devoted herself to her career, her church, and to others.

She still has complaints about life, her job, her body aching, and sometimes about how young our church is. Yet, when she worships, I am moved. When she amens, I am grateful. When she corrects me, I am humbled. When she contemplates, I slow down. When she makes suggestions, I shut up. When she reminds me, I take inventory. She is satisfied and has made the best of her circumstance. Whether well-fed, poor, abused, cold, humbled, lonely, searching, waiting, or sad, this is a woman who knows contentment. I want to be more like my friend, and I know her crown in glory will be larger than most, yet she will gladly and quickly lay it down. Oh yeah, one more thing: My wife and I always tell her we love her, but she won't say it back. I know she loves us though; she's just afraid to say it in case God moves her on. I pray against it daily.

In a culture that is obsessed with the next thing—the next fad, the next brand, the next relationship, the next church, and the next sensation—there's something beautiful about staying still and being grateful. Realizing that my life is not my own and that I am a child of God is extraordinarily comforting because it takes the pressure off. I'm satisfied with who I am and what I have, right now! It doesn't mean I'm not pressing on for more; but while I'm getting there, I can worship with a glad heart and a settled spirit. No matter what you've been through or are going through now, assume a posture of peace and remember my friend's story. If she can worship with gladness and live with peace, hope, and satisfaction, then I believe you can too.

TOUGH SKIN, SOFT HEART, AND BIG DREAMS

Do you remember the TV show *Friday Night Lights*? I enjoyed the series and took something from it. The team's mantra was "Clear eyes, full hearts, can't lose!" (#TexasForever). Coach

Taylor would repeat it to the team and the players would say it together as practice was ending or before they played a game.

I really liked it and implemented it with my son. When I pray over him at night, I say, "Tough skin, soft heart, big dreams." I'm speaking over him the thought that although you can't control all your situations, you can practice having tough skin (confidence/identity), a soft heart (humility/love), and big dreams (faith/goals). If you keep these three motivators in front of you, you can be driven and satisfied at the same time, which is necessary for peace with yourself and health with others.

Let's finish this chapter by saying these out loud over yourself:

Tough Skin: Be confident in who you are, discover your identity, and be grateful for what you have been given and especially what you haven't been given. This breeds opportunity to create and innovate. Two scriptures to stand on are 1 Thessalonians 5:18, "Be thankful in all circumstances, this is God's will for you" (paraphrase), and Galatians 3:26, "I'm a son of God through faith" (paraphrase). There's simply no reason not to have tough skin, for you've been given so much, and you have sonship access.

Soft Heart: Whether you win or lose, stay humble. Both winning and losing are necessary for our development and satisfaction. In fact, losing often teaches us more than winning does. We must be vigilant about keeping a soft heart so that we can worship in our pain, love through our disappointments, and have hope in the midst of crisis. I love what Tim Keller says: "If our identity is in our work, rather than Christ, success will go to our heads, and failure will go to our hearts."[4]

Big Dreams: Every single day is a gift. The scriptures remind us that "there isn't a promise of tomorrow," so in my opinion, we better seize today! For clarity, if you're a dreamer but don't take action, then you might as well just stay asleep. Still, remember that every great movement, every song written, every innovation or invention, every church started, every dollar made—everything begins as a dream and a vision! No matter how many times you get knocked down, *dream again.* You will find beautiful identity when you dream and hear the voice of God. We need our own dreams or we will regurgitate someone else's vision, voice, and calling, and that's when we experience misery and dissatisfaction. Dream again and then get up and do something!

4. "Redefining Work—Tim Keller (TGC13 Faith at Work Post-Conference)," *Vimeo*, May 3, 2013. vimeo.com/65391445.

CHAPTER 3

DON'T WASTE YOUR WAIT

"Patience is not simply the ability to wait—it's how we behave while we're waiting."
-Joyce Meyer

I hate waiting. I will do anything and everything to avoid waiting. I have broken the law to avoid waiting (like speeding and skipping lines at theme parks). Stop judging! I'll spend unnecessary money so that I don't have to wait—getting an Uber, ordering food instead of cooking it, or buying coffee instead of making it at home. I've left great sporting games too early because I wanted to beat the traffic and then something amazing happened at the end. I've also made a life out of waiting on my wife. I mean, how long does it take to do hair and makeup? Can't she just put a hat on? Whenever we're getting ready, I always sing to my wife an old Musiq SoulChild song, but I adjust it at the end:

I'll still love you if your hair turns gray, I'll still love if you gain a little weight. The way I feel for you will always be the same, *just as long as you hurry up*. I was meant for you and you were meant for me, yeah. And I'll make sure that I'll be everything you need, girl, the way we are is how it's always gonna be, *just as long as you hurry up* . . .

I know every husband is standing up and shouting me down right now. Clearly I'm joking; but the point is, life is full of waiting, and what we do with the wait makes all the difference. This first section of this book is all about getting *you* leveled up and ready for healthy relationships, and whether you like it or not, waiting is a discipline that no one really wants to talk about, preach about, or live. However, life's greatest blessings and most significant breakthroughs come after a season of waiting and persevering. I know many of you are wondering when you're going to meet Mr. or Mrs. Right. Wondering when you're going to make some solid friends. Wondering when you're going to get promoted at work. Wondering when your dream is going to be realized. How many times have we given up right before the breakthrough comes or before we see what we've been believing for? The best things in life come unexpectedly and often take longer than we want. It's a process of pruning and preparing. I'm reminded of God giving Jeremiah a vision:

> The Lord gave another message to Jeremiah. He said, "Go down to the potter's shop, and I will speak to you there." So I did as he told me and found the potter working at his wheel. But the jar he was making did not turn out as he had hoped, so he crushed it into a lump of clay again and started over. Then the Lord gave me this message: "O Israel, can I not do to you as this potter has done to his clay? As the clay is in

the potter's hand, so are you in my hand." (Jeremiah 18:1-6, NLT)

God is in the business of making beautiful things out of major messes. This process is messy, tedious, and extended. This scriptural illustration is likely a reflection of your life and is connected to your future. The potter is masterfully identifying the areas of us that are chipped and need reworking, and sometimes He even has to start over. You may feel like you have to start over and you can feel the crushing, pressing, and developing. Don't quit, friend, but let God do the work. When He is finished with you, you are going to be a beautiful piece of art adding outrageous value to those around you. The question becomes "What do I do in the meantime, while I'm formed into His image?" I'm so glad you asked.

TRUST THE PROCESS

As you can tell by now, I'm a huge sports fan. Well, I'm a Philadelphia sports fan mainly, and I like the stigma that comes with it. I'm proud we threw batteries and snowballs at Santa. He deserved it. I'm glad we boo everyone. I'm glad we're underdogs, even when we win. I'm glad nobody likes us and we don't care. Get over it!

Several years ago, the Philadelphia 76ers were tired of mediocre seasons in which they'd get the seventh or eighth seed in the playoffs and lose in the first round. So, they did something extremely controversial and ethically questionable—they started to "tank" (lose on purpose) and did it for years. The original General Manager and architect of this plan, Sam Hinkie, was quoted in May 2013 as saying, "We talk a lot about process—not outcome—and trying to consistently take all the best information you can and consistently make good decisions. Sometimes they work and sometimes they don't, but you reevaluate them all."[5] In the spring of 2015, the phrase "trust the process" officially landed and so it began to *build* something great.

I find the quote "we talk a lot about process, not outcome" incredibly striking. Why? Well, I want outcome and results so badly. I am obsessed with them, and if you're being honest, you probably are too. We want to get to the other side—to walking down the aisle, to the kids and family, to the degree, to the job, to the destination—so badly that we forget *the journey is where we attain the necessary equipment to sustain the destination.* God does so much work during the journey. If we don't trust the process, we will miss out on some of life's most valuable lessons, deepest fulfillments, and fascinating stories. *We might need the process more than we need the destination.*

You remember the story of Joseph? He was the favorite son of his father, Jacob. He was given a coat of many colors, had a bunch of "weird" dreams, told his brothers about them, and they tried to kill him. However, their consciences got the best of them, and instead of killing him, they sold him into slavery. That's where we pick up:

> When Joseph was taken to Egypt by the Ishmaelite traders, he was purchased by Potiphar, an Egyptian officer. Potiphar was captain of the guard for Pharaoh, the king of Egypt. The

5. Max Rappaport, "The Definitive History of 'Trust the Process'" (August 23, 2017).

Lord was with Joseph, *so he succeeded in everything he did as he served in the home of his Egyptian master*. Potiphar noticed this and realized that the Lord was with Joseph, giving him success in everything he did. This pleased Potiphar, so he soon made Joseph his personal attendant. He put him in charge of his entire household and everything he owned. (Genesis 39:1-4, NLT, emphasis added)

Joseph was *good* even when things were *bad*, and he was *faithful* even when his dream seemed *impossible*! He learned the secret of what to do while we wait. Not everything we are called to do or go through is fun, but it is purposeful! Wouldn't you rather have purpose over comfort? I recommend we live in such a way that we don't give up or give in until the dream of our heart becomes the reality of our life!

Here are a few more things we can learn from Joseph's life while we *wait* on God and trust His process.

SERVING AND SUCCEEDING ARE OFTEN SYNONYMOUS

Joseph could have thrown in the towel and been frustrated that he now had a master. Yet, he chose to sow a seed of service instead of a seed of discourse. *If you don't learn to embrace serving, you won't be adaptable enough to succeed.* Serving God and others while you *wait* on your increase or breakthrough is a fantastic discipline to practice and it will occupy your time with valuable opportunities and training.

After high school, I forwent university and instead interned at my home church in our youth department. I remember my first assignment as an intern; it was brutal. My pastor had me make a sign for the lobby, which turned into an arts and craft project. I was both frustrated and confused, particularly because I can barely write my name in cursive let alone create an artsy sign. After two or three different sign iterations that he didn't accept, I was even more frustrated and wondered why I was making signs to begin with. I also questioned why they were making me run to the local grocery store to pick up danishes and Sunday morning treats for guests. Not to mention, I was also driving pastors from airports to meetings and lunches all day long. I could sense resentment and bitterness welling up inside, and I was thinking, *I didn't come here for this! I came to learn how to preach, to lead worship, to be on stage!* Isn't it funny that when certain things aren't "going your way" you start to think about all the other things that are "wrong" as well?

I'm grateful my pastor was smarter than I was and had wisdom beyond my entitled years. He was subconsciously teaching me that if I was too big to serve, then I would be too *small* to ever lead. God started to speak to me that *I was not a slave; I was an investor.* What we see as slavery, God sees as seed. What I sowed then I would reap later. I could never hold a mic until I learned to gladly make a sign! Some of us view our jobs as slavery, our bosses as masters, our families and spouses as traps. Some of us view our role in church as just a number, our singleness as a curse, or our disability as a limitation. These are outright lies of the enemy. We must recognize that the potter is at work, we are the clay, and He has our dreams and His kingdom in mind. I believe the seed of service you sow today will reap a harvest of purpose and position tomorrow: "You did not choose me, but I chose you and appointed you that you should go and bear fruit" (John 15:16, NIV).

With this in mind, why don't you try serving while you wait? You might bear fruit you never dreamed possible or meet the necessary people you've longed to know or needed to have.

INTEGRITY WON'T GET YOU THERE FAST, BUT IT WILL GET YOU THERE WHOLE

Joseph was a very handsome and well-built young man, and Potiphar's wife soon began to look at him lustfully. "Come and sleep with me," she demanded. But Joseph refused. "Look," he told her, "my master trusts me with everything in his entire household. No one here has more authority than I do. He has held back nothing from me except you, because you are his wife. How could I do such a wicked thing? It would be a great sin against God." She kept putting pressure on Joseph day after day, but he refused to sleep with her, and he kept out of her way as much as possible. One day, however, no one else was around when he went in to do his work. She came and grabbed him by his cloak, demanding, "Come on, sleep with me!" Joseph tore himself away, but he left his cloak in her hand as he ran from the house. Potiphar was furious when he heard his wife's story about how Joseph had treated her. So he took Joseph and threw him into the prison where the king's prisoners were held, and there he remained. (Genesis 39:6b-12,19-20, NLT)

Here's another unfair scenario for Joseph to face, yet he does it with grace and extreme integrity. If I were him, I'd be cursing everybody, denying it, and putting up a riot. Yet, with humility and gentleness, he trusted the process. Joseph displayed a remarkable ability to not curse his enemies; instead, he leveraged them. Martin Luther King, Jr. said, "Never succumb to the temptation of bitterness." That's tough, but *there's usually a link between experiencing human injustice and walking out your God journey.* This is because God wants to position us to be blessed and practice faith, and these temptations often develop integrity and produce extraordinary fruit in our lives.

Martin Luther King Jr. once said,

> A person who constantly calls attention to his trials and sufferings is in danger of developing a martyr complex and of making others feel that he is consciously seeking sympathy. It is possible for one to be self-centered in his self-denial and self-righteous in his self-sacrifice. So I am always reluctant to refer to my personal sacrifices. But I feel somewhat justified in mentioning them in this article because of the influence they have had in shaping my thinking. I have been arrested five times and in 1960 put in Alabama jails. My home has been bombed twice. A day seldom passes that my family and I are not the recipients of threats of death. I have been the victim of a near fatal stabbing. So in a real sense I have been battered by the storms of persecution. I must admit that at times I have felt that I could no longer bear such a heavy burden, and have been tempted to retreat to a more quiet and serene life. But every time such a temptation appeared, something came to strengthen and sustain my determination. I have learned now that the Master's burden is light precisely when we take his yoke upon us.[6]

6. Martin Luther King, Jr., "Suffering and Faith," *Christian Century*, 510, April 27, 1960.

King's legacy lives on; his purpose was fulfilled even when his dream seemed impossible! We should never underestimate the power of a lifestyle of integrity. Who we are when no one is watching is what separates greatness from insignificance. For Joseph, Paul and Silas, MLK, and maybe you, the jail cell might be the most important place for destiny.

THOSE WITH UNRELENTING FAITHFULNESS EXPERIENCE UNREASONABLE FAVOR

But the LORD was with Joseph in the prison and showed him his faithful love. And the LORD made Joseph a favorite with the prison warden. Before long, the warden put Joseph in charge of all the other prisoners and over everything that happened in the prison. The warden had no more worries, because Joseph took care of everything. The LORD was with him and caused everything he did to succeed. (Genesis 39:21-23, NLT)

Joseph finds himself in charge *again* in the most unlikely scenario. Wow! We should never use our circumstances as an excuse not to excel. We have determination, fortitude, and grit at our disposal and we should use them so that we can make unlikely progress.

I sometimes wonder why some people experience continual progress and success and some don't. I've read multiple articles by both secular and Christian writers about what it takes to succeed, and here are the four main themes that arise as I balance those thoughts and my own experiences:

1. Consistent persistence
2. Teachability and adaptability

3. Mental fortitude
4. Working hard on the right things

Scripture tells us, "A faithful man will abound with blessings, but whoever hastens to be rich will not go unpunished" (Proverbs 28:20, NLT).

You need to know that there is no such thing as a get-rich-quick, get-success-quick, or get-position-quick scheme. *Be radically faithful now and find unreasonable favor later.* Why don't you try being faithful *where* you are and *with* what you have?

The story of Joseph is so fascinating because he ends up getting out of jail and becoming second in command of Egypt. Most important, his relationships with his brothers and father end up getting restored, too. All the dreams Joseph saw as a young man were realized. It's almost like God allowed the heartache and challenges of his process to take place so that he would be prepared when his dreams finally came to pass. The reality is, Joseph wouldn't have been able to handle knowing the full meaning of the dreams when he was younger because the process was necessary. Imagine Joseph twiddling his thumbs waiting to be in charge. Don't you get it? God is so gracious that He limits what we know and understand about the future so that we don't mess up the present. It's our responsibility to not waste our wait, and it's His responsibility to bring about the purpose in His timing.

You can read the rest of the story in the book of Genesis. One thing I want to focus on as we conclude this chapter is the fact that God has not forgotten about your dream. He's the one who gave it to you, so trust Him. Remember, waiting will often reveal our true motives and character. Joseph never manipulated God or man; he simply waited on his Redeemer. I hate it and I love it, but *God reveals our purpose and prepares His servants in a slow-cooker, not a microwave.* This is how God takes us higher. Think about it:

- Abraham waited—25 years for his promised son
- Noah waited—120 years for the rains to fall
- Jacob waited—14 years to have Rachel
- Joseph waited—14 years in prison for a crime he didn't commit
- Job waited—60-70 years for God's justice
- David waited—20 years to become king
- Simeon waited—his entire life to see the Messiah he was promised
- Hannah waited—19 years for her son Samuel
- Hosea waited—on his wife to stop being unfaithful
- 120 apostles and disciples waited—weeks or months in an upper room for the Holy Spirit

These few examples from scripture show us that these people were not passive; rather, they were active! They did not waste their wait, and neither should you. Serve, have integrity, be faithful, and wait on God for all He has shown you. The relationships you need and long for often intersect through your journey of faithful waiting. Joseph experienced restoration in his family after many years. If God can do it for him, then He can do it for you. On the other side of your willingness to level up your patience game is the chance to live your best life now and tomorrow.

PART 2

ROMANCING

CHAPTER 4

WHAT IS DATING, ANYWAY?

"I don't have a girlfriend, but I do know a woman who would be mad at me for saying that."
-Mitch Hedberg

Do you ever forget your first love, first kiss, or first heartbreak? Nope! It was the sixth grade and I was caught up. A young lady had just arrived at my small Christian school and I knew immediately she was the "one." My first kiss, I kid you not, was after youth group on the church property. Do you think I'll still make it to heaven? Doubtful. Now, while I'd like to say I had a strong pickup line and a great story about how I captured her heart for eternity, it didn't quite go like that. In fact, she broke my heart and set my life back for the next twenty years! Okay, I'm kidding. I recovered quickly and found another lady shortly thereafter.

All joking aside, many of us have experienced what began as a seemingly innocent relationship that later turned toxic. I recently counseled a young man who got caught up in a chaotic relationship built on the wrong infrastructure. He got the girl he was dating pregnant and their parents pressured them to get married quickly (sometimes a mistake we make in Christian culture). Eventually, though, they could not reconcile the deep canyon their unready lives had forged and eventually they divorced. The pain left in the wake of this divorce has taken years to heal, and now for a lifetime a child has to manage the tension of Mom and Dad living in separate places. Thankfully, God can heal and turn any wreckage into something hopeful. I'm happy to report this process is well underway in this situation.

You would be surprised how many couples I sit with who are convinced that one meeting with the pastor is going to fix decades of baggage and years of bad habits in their dating relationships. A few weeks ago, I sat in a coffee shop with a couple that were on a "break" because the guy cheated and the girl wanted to take him back but was afraid. Well, yeah! I'd be afraid too! However, the more I dug into their situation, the better I understood both sides.

He had an alcoholic mother whose actions when he was young built up an underlying resentment toward women. When a woman would make him angry, he would intentionally cheat to hurt her. The girl in this situation had been abused and abandoned as a child, and his cheating reopened an old wound. Even more heartbreaking, it triggered her defense mechanism—she was pushing him away because she was afraid he would abandon her.

As they cried together in public awkwardly, he confessed that he really loved this girl and wanted to marry her. I believed him. He just didn't know how. He also admitted that the way he makes money is, well, illegal and she's not entirely ecstatic about bringing children into his lifestyle that he seems unwilling to give up.

Doesn't all of this just sound insane? The reality is, these complications are so much more common than we think. History. Baggage. Lies. Unwillingness to change. It's all there, and it contributes to failed relationships and marriages over and over again. I will say, I'm proud of them for pursuing help and I believe they can make it. That's my prayer.

Over the next several chapters, I will share both laughable and heartbreaking stories as well as some insightful tips to help you cultivate healthy romantic relationships. I will also illuminate how to avoid hazardous relationships and will teach the art of honorably breaking away from harmful romances in your life. Before we dive into the practicals, it's important to set a precedent to the overarching purpose of "dating."

WHERE DID DATING COME FROM?

"The word 'date' was coined—inadvertently, it seems—by George Ade, a columnist for the Chicago Record, in 1896. In a column about 'working class lives,' he told of a clerk named Artie whose girlfriend was losing interest in him and beginning to see other men socially. When Artie confronts his fading love, he says, 'I s'pose the other boy's fillin' all my dates?'"[7]

7. Larry Getlen, "The fascinating history of how courtship became 'dating,'" *New York Post*, May 15, 2016.

COURTSHIP

Prior to modern dating, courtship involved one man and one woman spending intentional time together to evaluate marital possibility. The man and woman were usually members of the same community, and the courting was typically done in the woman's home under the watchful eye of her family, specifically her mother and brothers. Courting did not include sex, and divorce rates were lower before "modern dating" took over. As we see in the book of Ruth, Boaz technically "courted" Ruth and also sought counsel from the elders. While this method seems to be most effective, it is hard to imagine these rituals playing out in today's culture. I believe a hybrid of this model, mixed with modern dating, can be both biblically sound and culturally relevant enough to produce results.

MODERN DATING BEGINS

As the twentieth century began, increased wealth in the UK and US created more opportunity for fun, luxury, and entertainment. It was an electric time for many. Men could buy books with "sweet phrases" (aka, "pick-up lines") to use in attracting ladies to choose them over other men. We also see a gradual shift in sexual norms in the West. From the "flapper" movement of the Roaring '20s to the "free love" sexual revolution of the '60s, the question arose "Why would a man court and woo a woman when he could gain a chief benefit of marriage, namely sexual gratification, for free with no commitment?" This mindset eventually led to the contemporary example of "friends with benefits," and multiple sexual partners increased rapidly. Ambiguous commitments were on the rise and the hunt for sexual satisfaction outside of long-term commitment became normal and accepted as modern, necessary, and healthy.[8,9]

IT'S NOT WORKING

Ideally, healthy dating leads to healthy marriages, but this flow isn't necessarily happening. There are more divorces than ever, and statistics show that 64 percent of the population is single. As proven previously, being single isn't a bad thing. Sometimes it's safer. However, many desire a relationship and a family, and there is nothing wrong with that either. Yet, if we want a family, we need to learn how to date better so that when we do marry, our foundation is strong and able to sustain the rocky terrain of time. My hope is to lead the couple above toward reconciliation, legal income, healing from their past, and a promising future. They will have to level up if they want it.

A big question we should be asking ourselves is "Why are divorce rates so high?" Even within the church, they are above 30 percent.[10] Is it possible that we've done dating wrong and, in many cases, that has led us to do marriage wrong, too? I am convinced that we need a reset on how to cultivate romance for today's single. I believe there are timeless and universal truths regarding dating, but I also believe some of the rules have changed since

8. Skip Buzumato, "A Brief History of Courtship and Dating in America, Part 1," *Boundless*, October 16, 2018. www.boundless.org/relationships/a-brief-history-of-courtship-and-dating-in-america-part-1/.

9. Gert Hekma and Alain Giami, *Sexual Revolutions* (Palgrave Macmillan, 2014).

10. Bradley R. E. Wright, *Christians Are Hate-Filled Hypocrites . . . and Other Lies You've Been Told* (Minneapolis, MN: Bethany House, 2010), p. 133.

the clock of time has progressed. We need to level up and find the purpose of dating as well as an effective way to date in a very post-Christian culture.

INTERESTING STATS ON MODERN ROMANCE

Thirty percent of people are asked out on a date via text message. That's just funny and probably contributes to the confusing stat below.

Sixty-six percent of people don't know if they're on an actual date or just hanging out. I imagine that could contribute to anxiety and crossing physical lines too soon to figure it out.

The online dating industry revenue is over $1.5 billion. Did you know that only 66 percent of people on dating apps or who have online profiles go on actual dates? Maybe these companies intentionally try to keep people out of committed relationships so that they keep coming back to the online market. Who knows?

Seventy-three percent of Americans believe there is only one specific person for them out there, which is not biblical and could lead to missing out on a quality relationship in hopes of something better that doesn't exist.

According to a study by Nick Wolfinger, a sociologist at the University of Utah, people who get married between the ages of 28 and 32 are least likely to divorce.

Modern marriages have a divorce rate of between 40 and 50 percent. In other words, almost half of our homes are broken and many children are without two parents working as one unit.

Unmarried women account for 39.8 percent of all births. While some unwed fathers may still live in the home, it does create the potential for a large percentage of children to live without a consistent father figure.

Seventy-eight percent of reported rapes are date rapes.

Forty-five percent of dating-app users believe online dating is a more dangerous way to meet people, triggering fears and anxieties around dating.

Tinder users spend an average of 77 minutes a day using the app.

In the 1950s, there were 37.1 million more marrieds than singles, but according to the last census, that number has decreased to 12.1 million.

The number of Americans with no close friends has tripled since 1985[11], due in part to the increasing popularity of using the Internet to make interpersonal connections. Believe it or not, this inevitably causes us to be a little more awkward and less equipped to effectively take friendship to romance. Sometimes the best relationships come from the best friendships, and an inability to foster deep friendships can hurt long-term intimacy in the realm of romance.

THE PURPOSE OF DATING

I don't believe we're doing the dating thing the right way anymore. We have more apps, opportunities, and ways to connect; yet, fewer people are getting married, those who do are staying together for less time, and most are lonelier than ever.

---

11. Caroline Beaton, "Why Millennials Are Lonely," *Forbes*, March 7, 2017. www.forbes.com/sites/carolinebeaton/2017/02/09/why-millennials-are-lonely/#610181157c35.

What I will detail for you over the next few chapters is completely Christ-centered. So unless you desire a fully Christian value system in your life, you will absolutely disagree. With that said, whether you identify as a Christian or not, these principles are tried and true. You can apply these "rules" to your dating pursuit even now and find optimal success. For clarity though, *I believe* (according to biblical themes that I hope to prove) *the purpose of dating is to prepare for marriage, determine how to be married, and define who you want to marry.* There really is no other purpose. If you are dating because you're bored or lonely, it will lead to immorality, unhealthy dependence, possible stress, and probable heartbreak. Even when you are dating for marriage, heartbreak and disappointment may still be inevitable. In my opinion, the rules have changed, and this is why we need guidance and stronger resources around dating in the twenty-first century. C'mon, let's climb higher.

CHAPTER 5

THE TALK

"Give me chastity and continence, but not yet!"
-Saint Augustine

It was a sunny Florida afternoon during my eighth grade year. I had just sat down at the table for lunch and nothing could have been wrong in the universe—that is, until my mother threw a wallet and a pre-packaged condom at me (still no food on the table, mind you). She yelled angrily, "Do you know what this is?! Is this yours?!" Taken aback, I replied, "This is not my wallet, therefore, *not* my condom!" and I proceeded to remind her that "I don't have a wallet because you don't give me any money!" While the money statement wasn't entirely true, it was the quickest thought I had and I needed a strong response to the awkward flying objects that just landed in my lap. I finally did get to eat that day, but only after I had confirmed it wasn't my wallet and proven whose wallet (and condom) it was.

It's a funny story, but in reality many of us have no reference point for appropriate sex education in the home. Unfortunately, so many of us have only been educated by friends, media, or trial and error. I'm thankful (and so is my mother) that I grew up in a church that talked about sex in a biblical, tactful, gracious, creative, and calculated way. As I write, I'm reminded of a church in a major US city that has been given the privilege of teaching sex education in public schools throughout their entire county. They say, "We make this a priority, because what better way to learn sex education than in God's house or through God's people?" I echo that sentiment. Why? Because God invented it, it is best if we follow His instructions to experience the absolute fullness of it. Unfortunately, since the beginning of time, we've been complicating it. My goal for this chapter is to uncomplicate the purpose of sex.

Tim Keller says this: "If your god never disagrees with you, you might just be worshipping an idealized version of yourself."[12] It's very possible that what you're about to read will hurt, and I bet you might even disagree. But I promise, if you read with an open heart, it can set you free. "And you will know the truth [reality], and the truth will set you free [on a journey or process of freedom]" (John 8:32, NLT, brackets added for emphasis).

In Genesis, we read how God made Adam and Eve to dwell with Him in the Garden of Eden with a perfect design and plan ("Two shall become one") and they steward creation in perfect harmony—no shame, no guilt, no sin. While they had it all, Adam and Eve still messed it up. Because of their disobedience, the chaos of humanity ensues. Enter murder, jealousy, shame, fear, cancer, AIDS, STDs, sexual abuse, sexual confusion, and multiple partners. This goes on for centuries and God allows pain to inhabit humanity due to the choice given to Adam and Eve.

12. Timothy Keller, Twitter, September 12, 2014. twitter.com/timkellernyc/status/510458 013606739968?lang=en.

Ultimately, many of the Old Testament sin and lifestyle choices are disastrous on many levels, but in God's infinite mercy, He still lets us read it and learn from it, and He ends up using it for His glory. In the New Testament and for today, Jesus came to redeem *all* that was lost and broken. In the midst of our continued failures, Jesus is here to come near to our sinfulness and mistakes. It is fascinating that *this* God did not shun humanity based on our inconsistencies and impurities; rather, He ran toward us. This, of course, was God's resolution to and His eternal plan to draw His creation back to Himself. We see the Father's heart as He gives us what is most dear to Him (His Son) to have us again.

The picture of perfect harmony once again comes into view as Jesus surrenders in the garden in Luke 22:42 and says, "Not my will, but *your* will be done" (NLT). In turn, we (as the Church) are restored back to God and are given a much clearer interpretation and revelation of the scriptures. As we wade through this earth, we wait for Jesus to return for the Church (Christians) so that humanity can once again know pure pleasure, true worship, deep intimacy, and unending companionship. While we get bits and pieces of this on Earth, we will experience the fullness in heaven. All of this is *good news* and hope for those who have experienced sexual hardships or who have crossed lines that have separated them from God. In a moment, by one request, God can restore and make new all that was lost or torn apart.

Now, God's original design and continual intention for sex today is for you to experience a glimmer of this kind of security, pleasure, and companionship while on Earth. It is a good gift from our Father.

THE PURPOSES AND COMPLICATIONS OF SEX
(IN NO PARTICULAR ORDER)

1. Having Children

The first biblical purpose we see for sex in scripture is to establish the kingdom of God on Earth. We are, of course, talking about having children.

> Then God blessed them and said, "Be fruitful and multiply. Fill the earth and govern it. Reign over the fish in the sea, the birds in the sky, and all the animals that scurry along the ground." (Genesis 1:28, NLT)

Tim Keller says, "Sex is sacred because, with God, it co-creates a new soul. Sex propagates the human race. Its purpose is not merely for the building up of a family name. The purpose of sex is to create families of disciples, to establish new kingdom communities."[13]

When God says to "be fruitful and multiply, fill the earth and govern it," He is essentially saying to us, "Have sex in a responsible and purposeful way." More specifically, He is saying not to bring children into the world if you're not willing to disciple and raise them in the faith. Procreation is valuable so that we can continue building a kingdom society where the most good can be done on Earth, which means to populate the earth and fill humanity with heaven's love and the glories that the people of God are called to display.

The complications are obvious: when sex is not practiced inside the confines of responsibility, particularly a marriage

---

13. Tim Keller, "The Gospel and Sex," Redeemer City to City, essay, 2004.

relationship and a Christian worldview, then humanity experiences a plethora of challenges, such as the following:

- Parentless children
- A secularized culture
- Broken homes
- Confusion about identity and leadership roles
- The pressure of picking sides
- Generational iniquities, sin, and curses
- Incomplete sexual education
- A more difficult climate for discipleship

We believe, according to the apostle Paul's letters and the New Testament, that sex is most blessed, safe, and instructive for those in a God-recognized marriage relationship.

2. For Pleasure, Deeper Connection, and Fulfillment

The second biblical purpose of sex is for pleasure, connection, and marital fulfillment. *Sex is sacred and special because it is the analogy of Christ and the believer.*

First Corinthians 11:3 reads, "But I want you to realize that the head of every man is Christ, and the head of the woman is man, and the head of Christ is God" (NIV).

The Bible openly celebrates the power and pleasure of sex. Sex is supposed to be wonderful because it mirrors the eternal euphoria our souls will experience in heaven in our loving relationships with God, one another, and the final completion of the Bride and Groom united (the Church and Jesus). Proverbs 5:18-19 paints a beautiful picture of wedded ecstasy: "Let your wife be a fountain of blessing for you. Rejoice in the wife of your youth. She is a loving deer, a graceful doe. Let her breasts satisfy you always. May you always be captivated by her love" (NLT).

The Bible also explicitly details the delights of sex between a husband and wife in the Song of Solomon (but don't read until you're 18 years of age). In Song of Solomon 5:10-16, a woman boldly declares her physical attraction, sexual initiation, and deep passion for her husband. Written in an ancient time that was dominated by men, these poems are fascinating because there's no fear, shame, or shyness, only the sheer excitement of sex designed by God for humanity.

In his classic book *Mere Christianity*, C. S. Lewis states that the whole of God's creation, including the act of sexual intercourse, forms a beautiful dance where "plans without number interlock, and each movement becomes in its season the breaking into flower of the whole design to which all else had been directed."[14]

3. To Establish a Covenant

The third biblical purpose of sex is to establish a covenant. Every time you have sex, you are renewing a covenant. Unfortunately for many of us, we are simply enacting one. Tim Keller says, "The original purpose of sex was to 'become one flesh,' meaning a complete personal union. Sex creates deep intimacy, oneness, and communion between two people and God (Gen. 2:24; 4:14). In the Bible oneness is not simply a matter of emotion but is always the creation of a covenant."[15] A covenant is a life commitment, a deep and continual agreement between two parties of trust,

---

14. C. S. Lewis, *Mere Christianity*, Book 3, chapter 5.
15. Tim Keller, "The Gospel and Sex," Redeemer City to City, essay, 2004.

mercy, grace, love, and passion. We're not built for covenant with everybody because it's impossible to fulfill this level of promise.

If you can, picture your wedding day and the moment you got baptized with the knowledge of Christ as your Savior as the same type of covenant as you and your spouse. Now, picture the purpose of sex with your spouse like taking communion. We go into covenant with Jesus (hopefully once) and we renew and are reminded of that covenant through the ceremony of communion as regularly as appropriate. Such is with marriage and sex: you go into covenant when you say "I do" and you renew and are reminded of that covenant every time you are intimate with one another, from intercourse to everything in between. Therefore, even in your dating, be careful how intimate your kissing is. For many, bonding physically in this way is why some people stick with someone they have no future with because they simply cannot break away. Covenant has been established and deep emotional, chemical, and spiritual bonds have been built.

"Oneness" (sex), when done God's way, creates deep layers of vulnerability and unity and provides safe companionship. We see a biblical example of this in Song of Solomon: "On my bed night after night I sought him whom my soul loves" (Song of Solomon 3:1, NASB).

We also read, "For the wife does not have authority over her own body, but the husband does. Likewise the husband does not have authority over his own body, but the wife does" (1 Corinthians 7:4, ESV).

Although this is seen as repressive and offensive to "modernism" or "feminism," your body is not only *your* body: it's your spouse's and the Lord's. When a husband and wife mutually submit to one another, there is a healthy, cheerful, and careful responsibility to offer their bodies to each other. It should never be forced, dangerous, or used as a way to manipulate. *The purpose of intimacy in marriage is to treat your spouse's body as if it were your own—or more accurately, as if their body was on loan to you from God.*

The complications of sex outside its biblical purposes is that we were never meant to belong to many others but only to one. Sex ties you to whomever you are intimate with and they are tied to you. In fact, there are actually ten scientific health attributes for sex according to a *WebMd* article: it eases stress, improves sleep, may make prostate cancer less likely, lessens pain, lowers heart attack risk, counts as exercise, lowers blood pressure, improves women's bladder control, boosts libido, and helps the immune system.[16] This is fascinating and an important reminder that God is the ultimate scientist. When we do things the way He designed, it very much works to our benefit. However, when we function *outside* of God's design, things get messy and dangerous. *The very instruments that are constructed to help us can also end up injuring us when we don't heed the Master Architect's blueprints.*

When we take God's plan for sex out of order, the opposite of those benefits take place and, at times, cancel them out. For instance:

We have so much heartbreak. Ultimately, when you have sex with someone, your body is releasing a chemical called oxytocin.

16. Kara Mayer Robinson, "10 Surprising Health Benefits of Sex," WebMD. www.webmd.com/sex-relationships/guide/sex-and-health#1.

This chemical bonds and connects you to someone.[17] When sex is just casual or when not in a marital relationship, the chances of "unbonding" are higher, resulting in heartache.

We struggle to get over people. Have you heard of "rebound sex"? As a pastor, I've read up on the psychology behind this because I'm used to counseling people who want to rectify their bad decisions. One of the main issues with engaging sexually in order to get over someone is that it *doesn't work.* A rebound does not build our self-esteem, it usually doesn't make the ex jealous, it can hurt the feelings of your new fling, *and* it does not allow you to process the previous relationship. After it's over, you're left feeling even worse than before.

We sleep with anyone to feel close to them, but it never quite does the trick. Sleeping your way into love or babying your way into commitment doesn't really work.

We carry baggage from one relationship to the next and make someone pay for what they never did, leading to trust issues.

We can be infused with anger and bitterness over the disappointments of disconnected intimacy.

Our chances of disease increase. In 1983, there were no reported cases of chlamydia. In 1984, the CDC recorded 7,594 cases nationwide, and after 32 years of prevention efforts, reported chlamydial infections have reached an all-time high of 1,526,658 cases in 2015. That's an increase of 20,103 percent—not to mention expensive. Taxpayers spend $94,000,000 per year on STD prevention. Yikes![18]

17. Rita Watson, "Oxytocin: The Love and Trust Hormone Can Be Deceptive," *Psychology Today* (Sussex Publishers), October 14, 2014. www.psychologytoday.com/us/blog/love-and-gratitude/201310/oxytocin-the-love-and-trust-hormone-can-be-deceptive.
18. Scott Phelps, "STDs Are at an All-Time-High, but Liberals Are Ignoring the Only Proven Solution: Marriage," *LifeSiteNews*, December 23, 2016. www.lifesitenews.com/opinion/as-marriage-rates-decline-std-rates-rise1.

While God's way is the best way, it doesn't negate that it is also the difficult way. It is the road less traveled. It is also the most fruitful and navigable. "It won't be easy, but it will be worth it" is a phrase you'll hear in life from those who wished they did it God's way. Can God restore? Absolutely. Alternatively, we could decide to avoid the pain and baggage and try it God's way. He did create all this—for us.

REDEMPTIVE GOD

Many years ago, my dad received a flyer in the mail inviting our family to church. The flyer said that the pastor was going to be preaching about marriage, sex, and family. My father was intrigued because he had never heard a church discuss this topic before, so he decided to go. That night, in a small room with only a few hundred people, the pastor preached about these values and my dad gave his life to Christ. This same room is where I would later give my life to Jesus as well during a children's ministry service. My father had missed the mark many times in his life, he had lost his first wife and family, and my parents hadn't always done things in a biblical way. But that day God redeemed him in a thirty-five-minute sermon about marriage, sex, and family. Eventually, my mother gave her life to Jesus as well. Today, I'm a preacher, writing a book, and leading others to do the same. It is amazing to ponder that He can do that for you too, even as you read these pages. Redemption is here, because that's *who* God is. That's good news! Receive it.

CHAPTER 6

READY, SET, DATE!

> "Whenever I want a really nice meal, I start dating again."
> -Susan Healy

So far, I've given you a brief context for the purpose of dating and a more extensive explanation of the purposes of sex. In the next two chapters, I'm going to outline some strong recommendations for Christian dating. Heck, even if you aren't a Christian, I'm pretty confident the advice I'm going to give you will be incredibly helpful on your journey of love. I've titled this advice "The Definite Ds of Dating" just so you can have an obnoxious amount of alliteration and memorable statements. You're welcome.

IT'S ALWAYS DANGEROUS WHEN YOU GO HUNTING

Several years ago, the Vice President at the time (Dick Cheney) went on a hunting trip and accidentally shot his hunting partner. The birds were moving so fast as he was following them that his hunting partner got in the ricochet of the shot. The guy he shot said, "It's unbelievable that I hunted for as long as I had with no accidents whatsoever."[19]

Anytime you are pursuing prey and have a weapon, it's going to be dangerous. Hunting in and of itself isn't always bad, but without the necessary precautions and rules, it can be harmful. To recap, is dating wrong? No. While we cannot find a strong biblical precedent for it, pursuing people of interest isn't wrong, but it can be harmful if we aren't aware of the implications. Most particularly, we should be *spiritually aware, emotionally healthy,* and *engaged in godly priorities.*

Song of Songs says, "Don't excite love, don't stir it up, until the time is ripe—until you're ready" (2:7, MSG).

A great way to end up in a relationship is to intersect while both parties are pursuing Jesus, purpose, a career, and personal goals. In other words, I'm going in a positive direction, so are you, and we run into each other with common interests, spirituality, and value systems. I really believe the most attractive and "dateable" people are occupied with purpose, have jobs, and are confident in who they are.

If you are dating to be fulfilled and complete, you will be disappointed and frustrated every time. As we previously laid out, the truest purpose of dating or courtship is to determine if someone is going to be your life partner in a biblical marriage. Here are some reasons we should *not* date:

- Because we are lonely
- To test-drive vehicles (sex without commitment)
- To look or feel important

19. Meg Wagner, "Texas lawyer Dick Cheney shot 10 years ago goes hunting for the first time since accident—but he still hasn't gotten an apology from the former VP," nydaily-news.com, 2016.

- To fulfill a sexual need alone
- To add value to your life without understanding your own value

A good way to guard yourself against dating for the wrong reasons is to not go grocery shopping when you're hungry or go drinking when you're "thirsty." That's when anything will do and you'll get sick eating junk food or get a headache from getting drunk on cheap wine.

You may be asking, "Pastor Joey, what about dating apps?" We cannot be obsessed with these things. Timing and motive are important factors. There are some apps that are healthy and valuable and there are some that just aren't! You know which ones exist as "hook up" apps and the ones that exist for genuine connection. Choose wisely and ask trusted, godly people in your life for feedback. I also recommend when using these apps to check your motives and vet people thoroughly.

YOUR DESTINY HAS BOTH LITTLE TO DO WITH YOUR RELATIONSHIP STATUS AND EVERYTHING TO DO WITH YOUR RELATIONSHIP STATUS

As I wrote earlier, there is a significant place for singles in the kingdom and their singleness should not limit them from any opportunity of ministry, joy, or fullness of life. We cannot let culture lie to and steal from us. You've heard it said, "It's better to be single and wish you were married than married and wish you were single." Marrying the *wrong* person can take you down a path of limited effectiveness. (I'll get to what the wrong person looks like later.) I heard a preacher once say, "Don't marry someone for their potential; marry them for their patterns." I think that's extraordinary advice, because it acts as protection over your future. We can all think of friends who are wasting their time dating someone who has a few shining moments but then reverts to a constant cycle of questionable decisions. This preacher was suggesting that patterns are so much more telling than potential. Everyone has potential, but people worthy of your heart have healthy patterns.

I once knew a missionary who felt a strong call to a foreign nation, so he moved his family there to follow God's plan for his life. However, his wife couldn't handle the pressure of the mission field and wanted to take their kids back to the familiarity and comforts of the US. He then could not stay and fulfill his purpose; he had to put his family first and go home. Marriage and family become first priority after you say your wedding vows. You should know that your destiny is connected to your relationships. While I believe this former missionary is adding significant value to his family and his world, I imagine he often thinks of this missionary calling that he cannot fulfill. It's impossible to go back and wish to do it again, and I'm sure he wouldn't change the experiences he has had with his family. That said, wouldn't it be better to know what you're getting into before you get deeply committed and connected to someone? Don't give up your call for a relationship you "need" to have.

DEAL WITH YOUR ISSUES BEFORE YOU TAKE ON SOMEONE ELSE'S

I've counseled countless singles (especially teenagers) to start working on their own hopes, dreams, debt, and purposes before they dive into dating. Now, before I go further and sound like I'm anti-dating, I want to be clear. You can accomplish a lot with the right person, sometimes more than you can do alone. What I'm really talking about is the need to address some of your potentially damaging tendencies. We all have them. Whether you like it or not, emotionally connecting yourself to someone romantically requires you to help carry their burdens and support their dreams. Of course, having issues does not disqualify you from a relationship. However, if you're not aware of these issues, it may limit your effectiveness to maintain a healthy long-term relationship. The longer you go in a relationship, the less you'll be able to hide (and it's supposed to be that way). If you're unsure if you're healthy enough to date, here are some great ways to take inventory and find out:

- Go to counseling. Talk about your history and personality.
- Do you have a substance-abuse problem? If so, you shouldn't start dating.
- Are you freshly out of a relationship? If so, wait a bit.
- Do you have good friends and godly people around you to support you?

DISSOLVE PAST RELATIONSHIPS BEFORE DEVELOPING NEW ONES

This is one of my biggest pet peeves and a dangerous strategy the enemy uses to hurt us. We bounce from relationship to relationship and keep people hanging or lead people on in the event that who we're currently pursuing doesn't pan out. Jesus says, "Just say a simple, 'Yes, I will,' or 'No, I won't.' Anything beyond this is from the evil one" (Matthew 5:37, NLT).

Do not, I repeat, *do not* treat your brothers and sisters in Christ like this. Wait to date until you have dissolved your current defined or undefined relationship. Results may vary if you don't, including:

- Comparison
- Unforgiveness
- Rebound relationships
- Pain
- Destroyed friendships
- Vulnerable moments that lead to sexual sin
- Unhealthy patterns taken into the next relationship

If you give your heart to someone who hasn't dissolved their previous relationship(s), you are making yourself incredibly vulnerable and asking for unnecessary pain.

THE DECISIONS YOU MAKE TODAY WILL IMPACT YOUR RELATIONSHIPS TOMORROW

Every season of your life is a seed, and what you sow today you will reap tomorrow. God's mercy is limitless and He can restore any broken scenario. This doesn't mean there won't be unnecessary complications and work—particularly if you engage in sexual relationships with people you're dating. These complications have a tendency to appear later in your relational journey. According to an article in *Moral Revolution*:

We can't stop our bodies from doing what they were created to do. What were they created to do? Bond. We were created to connect with another human being in such a way that we would become one unit, together, for life. *Why does this happen?* Because our hormones cause us to glue, so-to-speak, with our partner. No amount of consent or informed decision making can change that. There's a bonding that occurs that supersedes a mere skin-to-skin connection. Scientifically, we know that sex engages us hormonally, neurologically, psychologically; it forms intense bonds mentally, emotionally, and physically, especially when we do it over and over again. "Scientifically, we know this: As we bond and break, bond and break, bond and break, we lose our ability to properly bond. When we're ready for that new, serious relationship or marriage, something is missing that prevents us from fully bonding; we don't feel that connected or committed. Our feelings may seem to diminish. When we see someone else a little more exciting, more appealing, more perfect for us, we're ready to move on in a heartbeat." Quite simply, any kind of sexual activity that takes place releases chemicals in our brains. . . . What makes things even more interesting is that these hormones are values-neutral. Whether it's a one-time encounter or a lifelong commitment, we bond the same way. It also crystallizes these emotional memories in our minds, making these encounters and experiences difficult to forget.[20]

In my opinion, this article exposes the significant challenges that engaging sexually before marriage poses. In fact, even in your future dating relationships, you can experience unnecessary problems associated with unhealthy decision making.

---

20. "The Invisible Effects of Sex Before Marriage?" *Moral Revolution.* www.moralrevolution.com/blog/the-invisible-effects-of-sex-before-marriage/.

There's a really solid couple who are friends of mine, but their dating journey was extraordinarily challenging. Paul tells us in Ephesians to love our wives as Christ loved the church, and this man truly loved his fiancée with this kind of patience. See, she had been in several unhealthy relationships prior to meeting him. Because of this, it was impossible to prove to her his love and commitment. She was constantly afraid of him cheating, leaving, lying, or abusing, so she put him under constant accusations and a number of unpassable tests. Fortunately, they got help and, through premarital counseling, much healing took place. Today there is a healthy and whole family forming, but it took more work than was entirely necessary to get there. Many times he almost walked away, but by the mercy of God, they worked it out. It's a sad truth for many people, but unhealthy relationships lead into the next ones, and her decision to stay in those patterns of unhealthy relationships almost cost her the best and right thing.

DEFINE THE VALUES OF YOUR HEART, PARAMETERS FOR YOUR MIND, AND BOUNDARIES FOR YOUR BODY BEFORE YOU DATE

And you shall love the Lord your God with all your heart and with all your soul and with all your mind and with all your strength. (Mark 12:30, ESV)

Heart: What are things that are important to you (e.g., marriage, kids, church, giving, serving, spirituality)?

Soul/Mind: There is always a chance that people in your life will be jealous and have something to say about who you date.

Some friends may push you to date toxic people and to break up with healthy people. Also, just because someone could be a wonderful, godly person, that doesn't necessarily mean they are the one for you. You should have discernment to know in your gut what's good for *you*. Listen to the *right* people who have your back and listen to the Holy Spirit. You have to be mentally tough to date in this day and age.

Body: Before you date, you need to have biblical clarity as to what is acceptable for you regarding limits of physicality—"work out your own salvation with fear and trembling" (Philippians 2:12, ESV). You should be able to communicate this and determine this before a relationship even begins. In the heat of the moment, it's hard to create a boundary. These must be predetermined before you commit to someone.

Do you have to determine and lay out everything you want before you go on a few dinner dates? No! That's weird and will freak someone out. However, before a relationship is defined, it's important to define some personal values and expectations.

DIFFERENT BLOOD DOESN'T BLEND

One day Abraham said to his oldest servant, the man in charge of his household, "Take an oath by putting your hand under my thigh. Swear by the LORD, the God of heaven and earth, that you will not allow my son to marry one of these local Canaanite women. Go instead to my homeland, to my relatives, and find a wife there for my son Isaac." (Genesis 24:2-4, NLT)

For clarity, I'm not talking about interracial relationships. God does not have an issue with this! I'm referring to spiritual blood-type. The implications here are that Abraham does not want his son to marry anyone outside the Jewish faith who is not a worshiper of Yahweh. He was so serious about it, he made his servant go into covenant with him.

Have you heard the scripture "do not be unequally yoked" from 2 Corinthians 6:14? The meaning of this verse comes from oxen being linked together by a bridle (yoke). If one ox is weaker than the other, the unevenness in weight is going to eventually break the bridle and the oxen may break their necks or resent each other. This is an illustration of what happens when we date outside of our Christian faith; it is dangerous and not recommended. Paul tells us in 1 Corinthians 6 to not team up with those who are unbelievers.

Don't flirt to convert or be a missionary to marry! If you're married to an unbeliever, pray for them and bring them to church with you. If you're dating an unbeliever, pray hard and seek godly counsel as to whether you should continue this relationship (yes, even if you have a child together).

CHAPTER 7

NOW THAT WE'RE TOGETHER

> "To keep your marriage brimming; With love in the loving cup . . . Whenever you're wrong admit it; Whenever you're right, shut up."
> –Ogden Nash

A preacher once said, "God's way determines what I'll do" and I simply love this statement. Why? Because it takes the pressure off of me having to figure out what to do, particularly regarding relationships. I believe God has so much to say to those of us who are in relationships and approaching long-term commitments; and if we'd just press into His Word and listen to His voice, we wouldn't have to make it up on our own or follow the example of other failed relationships. I really love what Peter says to us and it speaks that very line:

As God's obedient children, never again shape your lives by the desires that you followed when you didn't know better. Instead, shape your lives to become like the Holy One who called you. (1 Peter 1:14-15, TPT)

In other words, Peter reiterates that "God's way *should* determine what I do." For me personally, I want the Word and principles of God to form and shape my life, especially because it goes better when I do things the way He intended. He created the mind, heart, and emotions; therefore, His game plan for relationships must be better than mine. As we stated earlier, not everyone will experience romance or have a long-term journey with romantic love, but there are many who will. If you're reading this and thinking, *I won't ever date or be married* or *I've been married for so long, none of this applies*, then I encourage you to keep reading so that you know how to mentor those around you and remain inspired to thrive in your current relationships.

Regarding dating, it's impossible for you to remember all the "rules" and one-liners I've created for you in this chapter and the last. These ideas are simply guidelines, principles, and biblical themes to hide in your heart. I'm hoping you remember one or two when choosing and maintaining a relationship. Ultimately, we need the Holy Spirit to be in us and assist us in all things, especially romance. In every relationship, committing to God's way leads us to the most fruitful way of living. With that said, let's continue with part two of "The Definite *D*s of Dating" and discover what to do once you're *in* the relationship.

THE DETAILS OF WHO YOU ARE MAKE YOU THE RIGHT ONE

I don't believe there is *one* special person or "soulmate." Early Greek philosophers used that language, but there is no biblical context for it. The reason I've included this particular statement in the "now that you're dating" portion is because determining who the right one is takes clarity on what the right one means.

In the biblical story of Isaac and Rebekah, we see a beautiful picture of two people whose paths intersect. You can read the full story in Genesis 24, but here is the gist of it: Abraham was adamant that his son Isaac would find a wife who was a follower of God, a member of the Jewish faith. After making his servant swear to find such a woman, the servant embarked on the journey and God led him to Rebekah. She showed him kindness and generosity and was willing and ready to go back with the servant to marry Isaac and fulfill God's will. Some takeaways from this story are:

- The servant was looking not just for *beauty* but also for *heart*.
- She not only served *him* water but also *all* his camels.
- She was *hard-working, honoring, generous*, and a *servant*.

As Andy Stanley said, "Be the one who you're looking for is looking for."[21] Here are some good questions to ask yourself:

- How's your prayer and thought life?
- How's your serving-in-church life?
- How is your financial status?
- Do you have a vision for your life?
- Are you emotionally and spiritually ready (healthy) to be in a relationship?

Don't spend all your time *looking* for the right one—instead focus on *becoming* the right one!

21. Andy Stanley, "The New Rules for Love, Sex, and Dating," *North Point*, May 2011. northpoint.org/messages/the-new-rules-for-love-sex-and-dating.

YOUR EXPECTATIONS SHOULD DIRECT, NOT DEBILITATE

You *should* have expectations or minimum requirements while in a relationship, but don't set them so high that no one can meet them. For instance, saying, "He better have a six-figure job and six-pack abs!" or "Her age and her waist better be under twenty-six" are unreasonable and ridiculous, especially if you're still living with your mom and haven't worked out in years! They don't have to have *arrived*—but they should be *on their way*.

First Corinthians 9:24 says, "Isn't it obvious that all runners on the racetrack keep on running to win, but only one receives the victor's prize? Yet each one of you must run the race to be victorious" (TPT).

In other words, they don't have to have crossed the finish line, but they should at least be in the race. It is easy to have unrealistic expectations, and I know some people who are expecting their future significant other to be perfect. They won't be. They're not Jesus, and neither are you. Of course, this does *not* mean you can overlook glaring issues or make excuses for questionable behavior. I would recommend you make a list of what you are looking for so that you will know when you find it. In fact, I'd also make a list of your own traits and start with the flaws. Why? Sometimes there are things we expect or want out of people that cannot and do not exist. We want them to be our savior, but that isn't their role. And when they don't do the saving, answering, and fixing for you, you shut out someone who may have been very special and God-ordained.

GOING THE DISTANCE STARTS AND IS SUSTAINED
WITH FRIENDSHIP

Fun and friendship cannot be disconnected from relationships; they are the centerpieces! When I met my wife, Lauren, we were not automatically attracted to each other. However, once we spent time together, laughed together, and saw that we were both working toward a common goal, those romantic feelings began to bloom. We fell in love by having fun as friends first.

You and I were made for community (friendship) with each other. Things we have in common are the things that bring us together. When you find someone to be in a romantic relationship with, it is important to do life together, donate together, serve together, have hobbies together, and agree to pursue a common mission together. It is possible that if the fire is gone, it's probably because the friendship is too!

THE DIRTIER IT GETS, THE LESS YOU RECOGNIZE
GOD OR YOURSELF

Imagine that you are looking into a dirty mirror. Each time you spray a cleaning solution on the dirt, it causes it to streak. The dirt, grime, and liquid mix run down the mirror, obstructing your view even more. Each text you send that you know you shouldn't is a spray; each time you cross the line physically is a spray; the list goes on and on. Eventually, you can't see your face at all anymore and you begin to forget what you look like, causing you to lose a sense of who you are. *Sinful physicality will stunt your spiritual growth.* You begin to do things you never imagined yourself doing and wonder how you got there in the first place. It's not that God won't forgive you if you repent, but most find it hard to forgive themselves.

We see the damage that sinful relationships caused in King Solomon's life: "In Solomon's old age, they [his many wives] turned his heart to worship other gods instead of being completely faithful to the Lord his God, as his father, David, had been" (1 Kings 11:4, NLT).

Unfortunately, Solomon was incredibly unhappy and unfulfilled at the end of his life. He went on to write the book of Ecclesiastes in which he describes the meaningless nature of life. In my opinion, his life was one of unmet potential, as God gave Solomon the high gift of wisdom from above. Yet, his obsession with sexuality created a chasm between him and God that never quite mended.

DENIAL IS OFTEN A SYMPTOM OF A TOXIC RELATIONSHIP

I once had a dear friend who was in a toxic relationship with a girl who was not right for him. I questioned him constantly as to why he was dating her, which of course led to him becoming defensive and pushing me away. Because of his denial, our friendship, which was once joyful and life-giving, became strained and awkward. A way you can recognize a toxic relationship is when the areas in your life that once *gave* life become poisoned.

When you're losing friends, neglecting extracurricular activities, and hating everything that's not them, then it's time to get out of the relationship! In other words, when those who love you are on board, stay on the ship. When those who love you are jumping ship, get a lifeboat.

A significant other should complement you, not complete you.

DISCUSS THE DIRT

A small caveat to this section is that I'm using the word "dirt" as a figure of speech. In other words, the dirt may or may not be something bad, but it is something challenging to discuss with another person.

Now, imagine you've just sat down at a restaurant table for your first date with someone you've met online. The waiter comes to the table, senses the nerves of the new relationship, and asks if he can bring you something to drink. You unexpectedly respond by asking the waiter to come back in a few minutes, as you need a few questions answered before you proceed. He scrambles away awkwardly; then you ask your date, "Before we begin, do you have a criminal history? Also, how many sexual partners have you been with?" Based on their response, you plan to either stay or get up and walk away. Can you even imagine such a scenario?

There's absolutely a time and place for deeper conversations, and the further along your relationship progresses, some necessary relational history should be revealed. Although this can be difficult, it's fair to both of you to discuss each other's past and current struggles. After all, you'd never buy a house without knowing what the foundation is like. The deeper and more sensitive items (e.g., debt, sexual partners, criminal history, etc.) should come later. The reason being, it isn't fair to someone who may be a new creation in Christ to hold their past against them before you've given yourself a chance to fall in love with them. Am I saying that someone's past issues shouldn't keep you from a future with them? Possibly, unless they aren't taking the steps to rectify and deal with the trouble it may have caused. Yet, much can be worked through if you love someone, which is why premarital counseling should take place for any engaged couple.

By the way, right before Lauren and I got engaged, I found out that she was in a large amount of school debt. I wasn't happy at all, especially since I had worked hard to pay off school as I went. Even still, I loved her and sensed the Lord leading me to marry her. Had I known earlier in our relationship about her debt, I would have undoubtedly walked away. In another book, I'll share some of the miracles God has done with this, but for now I'm simply glad to say that I went through with marrying her and am grateful that we dealt with the "necessary dirt" further along in our journey.

DIP OUT WHEN DUMPED ON

When you get dumped, don't *become* a dump. Dumps are designated places for trash to be left to sit. You should value yourself enough to not become a dumping ground. If you let yourself become a dump, you only better your chances of letting them take advantage of you by getting back together when they miss you. This also goes for "taking a break," which sometimes happens in relationships where one or both parties feel like giving each other space. In my experience, when someone wants to take a break, it is their way of easing into the breakup. I don't often see relationships successfully come back together after a break, but it does happen. Sometimes we do need a break to clear our head and clarify if this relationship is what we want, and my advice to both parties is that if and when you take a break, *actually take a break.* If you're still texting that person and trying to stay in their life to remind them that you exist, it doesn't help your case, especially if they are the one who asked you for a break. Not respecting their space gives them no room to miss you or realize they do need you in their life.

The big question to ask when these circumstances arise is, do we trust God with our future, or do we trust our controlling nature more? Romans 8:28 is a pretty popular verse, often taken out of context. Paul says this: "And we know that for those who love God all things work together for good, for those who are called according to his purpose" (ESV).

Look, our definition of "good" is often different from what God sees as good. We think good is worldly gain of relationships, material things, status, and preferences. But sometimes good translates into momentary loss for the sake of eternal gain. There may be a very good purpose for this relationship ending or going on a break. That said, even though God has a purpose, He is still present in your pain. He doesn't gloss over your gloom and He doesn't shove aside your suffering. Jesus mourns with you in the night until the morning light comes. Trust and release control. If it's meant to be, don't get in the way of destiny; maybe they just need time. *God* plays a better matchmaker than your stalking does. In the meantime, pray for them and continue to work on becoming who *you* were meant to be.

FRIENDS WITH COUPONS?

One day when I was in eighth grade, I was hanging with two of my classmates. I said to my buddy, "You're so-and-so's boyfriend, right?" Of course, I was just trying to start a conversation and meet new people. He quickly jumped in and said that she was his "friend with coupons." Say what? While I had recently been kicked out of my Christian school and was now attending public school, I still had an element of innocence that didn't lend me to these cultural references. You may have heard this term as "friends with benefits." Later on, I realized that he meant he didn't want to be in a committed relationship and only wanted physical benefits without relational commitments. He told me he was from the "hood" and only had coupons to offer, no benefits. I chuckled when I heard it, but I always wondered how that comment and his actions made that girl feel. She was better than that, and so are you, especially if this is something you are allowing to take place in your own life.

Oftentimes when one party doesn't want to be committed, the other party who does want commitment allows these (in my opinion) relational abuses to take place. Sadly, we've bought into the lie that if we don't give them a part of us, they will never want us. However, when we allow others to have a portion of us without committing to us, it usually says more about how we view ourselves than it does about how we view the relationship. During your breaks, your breakups, or before someone is verbally (or socially) committed to you, engaging physically will only hurt your chances of something lasting long term. I've found that confidence and personal identity make you the most attractive and draw people to you, particularly in a romantic sense. Your willingness to give yourself away emotionally or physically, especially when there is no commitment, displays deep insecurities and opens you up to being taken advantage of. Those with bad intentions smell insecurities like sharks smell blood in the water. They will take advantage of your wounds and take what you're willing to offer until you have nothing left. In all of this, the more we remember what the psalmist wrote, the better shape we will be in. His prayer is like surgery to the wounded and insecure places of our lives:

> You made all the delicate, inner parts of my body and knit me together in my mother's womb. Thank you for making me so wonderfully complex! Your workmanship is marvelous—how well I know it. (Psalm 139:13-14, NLT)

If God has knit you together so wonderfully, then find peace with yourself whether dating, single, or on a break.

DETOX WHEN YOU GET DUMPED

Don't deny your pain and heartbreak; instead, give yourself time to heal after you've been cut. I've heard and seen many stories of people jumping right back into relationships after ending one so that they can fill the void that was left. I believe this is dangerous and a recipe for stunting personal growth. The time after a painful breakup is a rare opportunity to experience personal growth and perspective. Post-breakup is an amazing time to reflect, recognize where you may have made harmful decisions, potentially repent from areas in that relationship that affected your faith, and heal from natural hurt. Ecclesiastes 3 was written by the "wisest man to ever live" and he says throughout this chapter that there is a time for everything: a time to cry, a time to heal, a time for war, a time to laugh, a time for love, and on and on and on and on. Point is, there is also a time to pause after a relationship has ended. Why? Well, take a look at five things I've noticed that happen when we jump into relationships immediately after ending one:

1. Impossible expectations are put on the new person to heal us and provide for us like the previous person didn't. There are some voids that only the presence of God can fill. They are not our savior, but they can become our god if we are not careful.
2. Sometime we make the new person pay for what the previous person cost us.
3. We realize we didn't truly care for the new person but "needed them" to get through our heartache—causing both of us more pain later.
4. We don't heal from the previous relationship's hurts, so we lose the new person because we aren't whole enough to handle their health. They were ready; we were not. Now we've lost someone good because we weren't healed.
5. We lose ourselves and forget that we have dreams, an identity, and a purpose. Only space and time can remind us of the calling on our life.

C'mon, you're better than a rebound! Let's remember who we are—children of God, beautifully and wonderfully made. Things will work out for your good and God's purposes—for you will prevail. Relax. Rest. Recover. Level up.

IT'S DANGEROUS TO ACT MARRIED WHEN YOU AREN'T

I'm about to go there (not like I haven't gone there already in this book). This principle is one we overlook as an outdated rule that has zero cultural relevance. We've covered sex already, so you know where I stand and what I'm suggesting on that front. But there is a further issue at play that leads to problems later on. This, of course, is living together and delving into lifestyle intimacy before legally and spiritually ordaining marriage as a covenant before God. Here are some examples of what I'm talking about:

- Combining banks accounts before getting engaged
- Sharing big purchases, such as homes or vehicles
- Living together before marriage
- Having children together before marriage
- Sharing pets. Okay, kind of kidding, but who gets the dog if you break up?

By living together before marriage, you might end up potentially practicing an unnecessary divorce. If you have furniture, appliances, dishes, pets, etc., together, then what happens when you break up? Even if you are able to split material items, you've now experienced a divorce when you weren't even married in the first place. It's incredibly damaging to the body, soul, heart, and mind.

In our culture, marriage is becoming less and less frequent, and there are a variety of reasons for that. Divorce is one factor for sure, as are school debt and bad financial stewardship, the societal shift away from a traditional family, a post-Christian culture— and a lot of bad teaching from the church has played a part, too. In some ways, I get it. Moving in together makes life so much easier. We can split rent and save dollars because we're "eventually getting married anyway." And while that seems easier and makes financial sense, God's economy really doesn't make natural sense. In fact, it makes me think of John's words:

> Do not love this world nor the things it offers you, for when you love the world, you do not have the love of the Father in you. For the world offers only a craving for physical pleasure, a craving for everything we see, and pride in our achievements and possessions. These are not from the Father, but are from this world. And this world is fading away, along with everything that people crave. But anyone who does what pleases God will live forever. (1 John 2:15-17, NLT)

I believe with all of my heart that when we do things God's way, it's the absolute best way. His way should determine what I do, and when I steer away from this, consequences often ensue.

According to the Institute for Family Studies, statistics show us that the chances of divorce amongst couples who have never lived together are 20 percent in the first five years of marriage, compared to a whopping 62 percent amongst those who moved in together before marriage. That is *three* times more likely![22] Those "living together" also experience *higher stress* than those who are married, are three times more likely to experience infidelity,

22. LoveToKnow.com, Institute for Family Studies.

and report higher levels of depression as well as substance-abuse problems.

Recently, I watched a sermon from Pastor Michael Todd of Transformation Church in which he shared a beautiful recipe for relational progress. Essentially, he said this:

Single: Learn yourself and work on yourself (level up) while single and through relationships.

Intentional dating: Do it God's way and have boundaries and a strategy behind dating. Date while you date and date while you're married, too.

Engagement: This is a separate item and the finale of dating. Now, come together and begin to blend.

Marriage: Now act married and be married after the previous steps have been taken.

Love: This is my favorite step. He says that love really happens after you're married, not before. You don't know love until you really say no to yourself and meet someone else's need. Love is something that is discovered and grows deeper as you act out love. Long-term love is a choice you make. (Pastor Michael Todd's teaching series "Relationship Goals" is very much worth the watch.)

Children: Now that you know and have love, this is a good time to add kids into the mix. Otherwise, if the kids become a distraction to your business relationship or relational agreement, once they are gone, your relationship might be gone too. Having kids in their proper place helps ensure love beyond the kids.

Repeat: He closes by reminding us to repeat the process by going through the steps again. We must date our spouse, choose love and service again, continue to grow like we did when we were single, and reinforce our marriage before adding any other kids to the family.

These steps are gold and help us understand why it's so complicated and dangerous to act married when we aren't. If you do it God's way, by His design, the chances of reaching new heights in love increase quite significantly.

PART 3

FRIENDSHIP

CHAPTER 8

I NEED YOU, YOU NEED ME!

"My imaginary friend thinks he has a problem."
-Anonymous

Immediately after high school graduation, I interned for the church I grew up at in Orlando, Florida. I was studying to be a pastor, and one of my assignments was to host an interest-based small group. Naturally, I chose to lead a group on Saturdays where we played football and would discuss something from the sermon during our break.

Anyway, I met Eric and his brother Shawn one Saturday morning as they stumbled into the group (hungover or high, still not sure which) and we clicked right away. They had recently moved to Orlando and were renting an apartment near the church. They happened to have visited the previous Sunday and had seen a small-group sheet on the info table on their way out of church that listed my group. I had no idea at the time that this relationship would reap much fruit later in life, but that's just how God works.

Eric and Shawn were a mess. They were potheads, involved with other drugs and substances, had little direction for their life, and had no money. Shawn was in a nasty custody battle with his baby mama, and they also had a cat (no one needs a cat). I felt compelled to begin a relationship with these guys, to reach out and be their friend. So, I did. I remember getting Eric's phone number and going to pick him up to hang out one afternoon. I walked into a smelly room with a mattress on the floor, some covers, and barely anything else.

After a period of time, both Eric and Shawn committed their lives to Christ, got real jobs, plugged into our church, and started to productively contribute to both the friendship and our church community. I will say, the discipleship process, particularly with Eric, taught me so much about how to lead someone to victory, out of slavery, and toward something better than they even knew was possible. While Shawn eventually met an amazing woman, got married, acquired a stable job, bought a home, and had more kids, Eric recognized there was a call to ministry on his life and started to follow it. Eric is now married with a kid, is a church planter, and has had several successful ministry roles.

WE NEED EACH OTHER

A few things really stick out to me in this story and point to our subject of biblical community. Both of these boys taught me a ton about discipleship and how to care for people as a pastor. I needed them and their struggles to teach me how to disciple on a bigger and broader scale. While their lives overwhelmed me at the time, I now pray for the simplicity of their struggles as a lead pastor today. For me, they were a great starting point for the complications of people's lives I now deal with. As Christians, we are called and expected to care for people and walk with them toward victory. I'm so glad I learned how to do that with my friends, and I know for certain that God placed them and their troubles in my path.

Several years ago, while we were in the planning stages of starting our church, Eric was a youth pastor in Arizona and had me in to speak at his youth retreat. I preached for the retreat and stayed over to preach that Sunday morning for the adults. Eric's church took the single biggest offering for our new church plant we had ever received. Additionally and most importantly, I met a man that day who was on vacation with his family and had happened to "stumble" into Eric's church. This man, JD Pearring, leads a network that cares for and assists church planters. This introduction connected us to several sources of support and funding needed to start The Block Church (our church plant in Philadelphia, Pennsylvania).

Plus, through JD, I met Paul Taylor, another church planter and the lead pastor of Rivers Crossing Community Church in Cincinnati, Ohio. At that time I had been searching for a covering, for a pastor's pastor who was where I wanted to be. So, I pursued Paul and he took us in. Rivers Crossing has given us a great amount of resources and spiritual support to help The Block Church begin. I know Eric is reading this, laughing, secretly taking credit for everything. But I'll remind him and you that we need each other and God knows it. If I were in church right now, I'd tell you to look at your neighbor and tell them, "It's a set-up!"

Here's the part of this story that I find so special. Shawn and his wife, Jenny, have built an outstanding friendship with my parents. While Eric and I live in other states, my parents and Shawn's family stayed in Florida. Shawn has helped my parents with so many things around the house, cares for them as they grow older, and supports them as a son while I'm at a distance. My parents, in turn, have been second parents to Shawn and Jenny through ups and downs, tragedies, celebrations, and family gatherings. My parents love Shawn as much as (or more than) me, I'm convinced. My parents needed Shawn and Jenny, and Shawn and Jenny needed my parents. It's beautiful—it's a set-up.

THE DESIGN FOR COMMUNITY

In Genesis 2:18, the Bible says, "it's not good for man to be alone." In other words, God saw Adam and knew he needed a partner, a warrior teammate in stewarding life's glorious ups and downs. Woman coming from man (see Genesis 2:22) reminds us that we come from each other and belong to each other as well. Ironically, this principle reminds me of communion. Have you ever taken communion at church? I'm sure you have. I believe the act of communion is quite reflective of the function of Christian community and friendships. The early and original church didn't just take communion together; they *were* communion together. I'll explain.

> They devoted themselves to the apostles' teaching and to fellowship, to the breaking of bread and to prayer. Everyone was filled with awe at the many wonders and signs performed by the apostles. All the believers were together and had everything in common. They sold property and possessions to give to anyone who had need. Every day they continued to meet together in the temple courts. They broke

bread in their homes and ate together with glad and sincere hearts, praising God and enjoying the favor of all the people. And the Lord added to their number daily those who were being saved. (Acts 2:42-47, NIV)

Throughout history, the church has gathered and done these sacred things we just read about. She gathers to pray, learn, break bread, give, celebrate, and fellowship. The Lord's Supper did not appear as an isolated event but was part of something that took place throughout the ministry of Jesus. Eating meals and breaking bread were things Jesus did all throughout His ministry. Wolfgang Vondey suggests that *Jesus had established His community as a community of bread.* This was not uncommon for the Jew in a Greco-Roman world to do, as religious and social gatherings of the day often were centered on a common meal or banquet.[23] "Now as they were eating, Jesus took bread, and after blessing it broke it and gave it to the disciples" (Matthew 26:26, NLT).

The Hebrew word for blessing here is *berakah*.[24] This word refers to blessings of God universally, on all creation, and a posture of gratitude rather than a format of prayer. It also represents a spiritual way of life rather than ritual or exercise. Jesus is asking His followers to not just take part in a meal of remembrance or participate in a specific ritual prayer, but rather to live a life of blessing. Foley reminds, ". . . not only were they supposed to repeat his actions with bread and a cup of wine, but they were to continue living in the spirit of blessing [with each other]."

23. Wolfang Vondey, People of Bread: Rediscovering Ecclesiology, 2008.
24. "Berakah," *Encyclopædia Britannica*, January 14, 2018. www.britannica.com/topic/berakah.

Communion is the continuation of Jesus' ministry beyond His physical presence on Earth. This act focuses *not* on methodology or ritual but on a way of life that emphasizes empathy, companionship, unity, healthy conflict, blessing, and self-giving. Ultimately, biblical community means we are supposed to be living and sharing life together.

COMMUNITY IS ACCOUNTABILITY

The early church saw the importance of unity and the link between being reconciled with God and with our neighbor. With unity, companionship, and self-giving as primary themes, it was important for the community to be reconciled when necessary (we will address this piece more in a later chapter). However, look what Paul says in Romans:

> We who are strong ought to bear with the failings of the weak and not to please ourselves. Each of us should please our neighbors for their good, to build them up. For even Christ did not please himself but, as it is written: "The insults of those who insult you have fallen on me." (Romans 15:1-3, NIV)

This practice of breaking bread is continued here in the book of Acts, and Luke is not simply talking about regular meals. *Just as communion reminds us of our salvation, so too community reminds us of Christ's suffering.* As we suffer together and carry one another's burdens, we are reminded of what He did and what we are called to. *While communion reminds us to present ourselves in a worthy manner, relationships result in us becoming worthy.* How? Because true Christian community provides us with authenticity and raw honesty that spur us on to greater things.

For instance, you know how we post photos and stories online and make them look really creative? Or, more truly, how we try to cover all our imperfections by using filters? We're often afraid of people seeing the real us or knowing what we struggle with. Beautiful community doesn't have any filters. In fact, *the best communities are ones without filters, where honesty, honor, and vulnerability are the centerpieces.* This is why we desperately need godly community in our lives. It destroys filters (barriers) and fills us with the deepest joy.

Sadly, many run from any sort of honesty out of fear that the real us won't be accepted. When we are defensive or dishonest, we're only hurting ourselves. Community exists to keep us from putting on a facade. Vulnerability in friendship draws us deeper to God and guides us further toward truth. We cannot be afraid of opening up with other believers and we certainly should not run when trusted friends or mentors give us feedback on areas in our lives we can improve. Of course, we have to be smart and carefully navigate who we communicate with. However, using the hurts of the past or the gossip of others to keep us from experiencing one of the main purposes of the church limits some of the best things life has to offer. I dare you to embrace accountability and the fullness of Christian community. Don't run from it; run toward it and you will surely be glad you did.

As we close this chapter, remember that *Christian community done right is a beautiful mess, a mountain of work, and a necessary supplement for your growing journey with God.* We need each other and it's often a set-up for what we need on our journey. James explains this best when he says, "Confess your sins to each other and pray for each other so that you may be healed. The earnest prayer of a righteous person has great power and produces wonderful results" (James 5:16, NLT).

This verse is remarkable because it seems like God puts the power of healing in the hands of the community. James isn't saying that when we confess to each other we will be forgiven. No! Only God can do that. He is saying that when we confess to each other (our sin, our stuff, our struggle), we'll find healing. Could it be that God would release His healing power in the form of community, godly counsel, and friendship? And while it might be complicated to get messy with people, the reward is wholeness. I want that. Sign me up for community.

CHAPTER 9

NEW TEAM

"I love my computer because all my friends
live inside it."
-Anonymous

At the end of my freshman year of high school, I got called into the varsity football coach's office. He told me they were moving me up and, if I did well in practice, I'd skip the JV team and start on varsity. *Yikes!* The end of the year and summer went pretty well, so I stayed on the team. Enter sophomore year. While I was on the varsity team, the position I was playing had a Division 1 recruit in front of me. I was there to back him up and learn. This D1 recruit had a broken family and some major challenges at home. He was also very popular and I could tell he didn't like me much. I didn't do anything specific, but I suppose the threat of a sophomore didn't exactly please his highly touted preferences.

Anyway, this young man got in trouble early in the season and the coach was so fed up with him that he told me I'd be starting. What I haven't told you yet is that I was playing quarterback, so the pressures were pretty significant, especially since we were about to play a highly ranked team in Central Florida. On the way to the game that night on the bus, I nervously blurted out that if we won, everyone would have to come with me to church the following Wednesday night. Mind you, we were predicted to lose this game by 22 points. Miraculously, the first pass I threw was an 82-yard touchdown (I closed my eyes and threw it) and we ended up winning the game on a glorious field goal.

What happened over the next month was sheer insanity. The team started to go to church with me, we were winning our games, and even the newspapers and TV stations were covering our spiritual revival as a team. Oh yeah, and the hotshot who was in front of me? Well, he also started coming to church and we built a friendship that lasts to this day. I always joke that I'm responsible for his NFL career because we started to split time after that game and he moved to wide receiver, the position he plays now.

THE RIGHT TEAM IS EVERYTHING

The wildest part of this story is how God reconnected us over time and used this relationship to build His kingdom. Several years ago, Lauren and I were working at a church in the Midwest and my friend got traded to the Chicago Bears. We reconnected on Twitter, and he told me the team was between chaplains. So, for a year, I would go down to Chicago and preach for the Bears while getting to hang with my friend and his wife. This season was necessary and fruitful for both of us. He had recently reconnected to his faith and he and his wife needed our support on their journey. Additionally, he blessed me in ways he'll never fully know.

The most tangible blessing came not long after Lauren and I packed up everything we had and moved to Philly to start our church. We had saved enough money to live for a year and were prepared to give everything we had to start what God had put in our hearts. At this point, we had been in Philly for two months and had just rented a house. Because we didn't have jobs to prove our income, our landlord made us put down first month, last month, security deposit, *plus* six months of rent up front. In a single moment, nine months of our year's savings disappeared. Almost immediately after that, my friend sent us a very large check that served as a reminder to us that God had this thing and we would be okay. That check had way more to do with God's peace and faithfulness than it did a dollar amount. My friend doesn't even know all the people who will line up in heaven one day to thank him because he gave sacrificially. And to think, it all started with an invite to church in high school. Never underestimate a simple seed, because in due time, it will sprout. God is so faithful.

In my life, I've needed different people to be on my team to help me do what God called me to do. While my friend may not fully know it, he held my arms up in a special way. In Exodus 17:8-13, Moses is leading his people to fight a battle that seems impossible. He recognizes that the miraculous staff of God is really their only chance:

> While the people of Israel were still at Rephidim, the warriors of Amalek attacked them. Moses commanded Joshua, "Choose some men to go out and fight the army of Amalek for us. Tomorrow, I will stand at the top of the hill, holding the staff of God in my hand." So Joshua did what Moses had commanded and fought the army of Amalek. Meanwhile, Moses, Aaron, and Hur climbed to the top of a nearby hill. As long as Moses held up the staff in his hand, the Israelites

had the advantage. But whenever he dropped his hand, the Amalekites gained the advantage. Moses' arms soon became so tired he could no longer hold them up. So Aaron and Hur found a stone for him to sit on. Then they stood on each side of Moses, holding up his hands. So his hands held steady until sunset. As a result, Joshua overwhelmed the army of Amalek in battle. (NLT)

Now, before I go any further, you may be thinking, *Who were Aaron and Hur?* Hur is simply described as a companion of Moses (a friend, teammate, or servant) and he was from the tribe of Judah. In other words, he was from the *same value system*. Aaron was Moses' older brother, and during the Exodus he did all the speaking for Moses, who had a speech impediment. They were connected by blood and heart. These men were Moses' "team."

A team exists to help us accomplish all we are meant to do. These teammates can be friends, family, or strategic relationships that we've stewarded well and are reaping a return. *Is it possible that we might have a team but not the right team?* Yes. But if we want the right results in our lives, we need to be surrounded by the right team, with the right values, who have our best interest at heart. The Word says, "Do not be misled: 'Bad company corrupts good character'" (1 Corinthians 15:33, NIV).

WHAT DOES THE RIGHT TEAM DO?

The right team provides security and a strong foundation. As we read in Exodus 17, Aaron and Hur found a stone for Moses to sit on when he became tired. Think about what the stone represents: it is a safe and secure foundation for us to continue the work God has called us to, reminding us that we cannot do it alone and were never meant to!

WHO IN YOUR LIFE PROVIDES A SECURE FOUNDATION FOR YOU?

When you identify these people, create more space, time, and vulnerability for these relationships. If you don't have these teammates, be that for someone else. A friend once told me, "I've never been one, but I want to be a best man in someone's wedding." I responded, "If you want to be a best man, you have to be a best man."

Think about it: we only have what we are willing to sow. If you desire or need something, do or be that for others. On the other hand, If someone provides an unstable environment for you, or you realize you provide an unstable environment for others, begin to remove yourself from these relationships or pause to reflect on how your actions are hurting others. There are simply some people who don't belong in your life. (Later, I will explain how to appropriately transition away from those relationships.) For clarity, if you're married and not under physical abuse or infidelity, pursuing counseling to shore up insecure foundations may be necessary.

ENCOURAGEMENT AND ACCOUNTABILITY

"Then they stood on each side of Moses . . ."

When I visualize this image, I imagine Aaron and Hur standing beside Moses, reminding him that he still has a job to do. The text doesn't say this explicitly, but why else are they there? There's a battle going on and Moses is fighting for his life. *Good, godly relationships will fight with you, for you, and around you—never against you.* The right team will provide encouragement and accountability!

There's a saying that we are the average of the five people we spend the most time with. So why are we spending time with Miss Badmouth, Mr. Unmotivated, Mr. and Mrs. Always-broke, Sir No-vision, Boy Lazy, Lady Bitter, Dude "I can't keep a job or even want one," Girl "I have no morals," or Bro who "puts pressure on you to do this or that, but none of it gets you anywhere except *all the above*." If that's you, it's time to get some Aarons and Hurs in your life! Surround yourself with people who challenge you, push you, question you (in love), are further along than you, sharpen you, inspire you, motivate you, don't pressure you to compromise or sin, and who want to see you win *your* battle, not just get help with theirs.

In college, I was assigned to lead a youth camp in Arizona one summer. It was there that I met GraceAnn, a girl from my college who was from Flagstaff. We were supposed to be co-leaders for recreation, but she ended up being my assistant all summer. I remember how fun that summer was and how I would make Grace incredibly uncomfortable by making her get on the mic and lead things she had never led before. She hated me and loved me at the same time, and our relationship is the same today. She gets mad at me for making her stretch and grow but loves me for it after the fact.

Can I tell you how strategic God is? Grace and I built a friendship that summer that has lasted for over ten years. When we were starting the church, Grace was one of my first calls. I said, "Grace, you want to be a missionary? Well, no better place than Philly to fulfill that call!" I also told her, "I can't do this without you." And it was true. As I write this book, Grace leads one of our locations and stands on both Lauren's and my side, encouraging and fighting alongside us. I tend to get a lot of credit because of her faithfulness and friendship. Now do you understand why you need a good team?

PROVIDES STRENGTH AND REMINDERS

"... holding up his hands. So his hands held steady until sunset   ."

This moment is a picture of the cross. In the middle is Moses holding a wooden stick, to his left is mercy, and on his right is grace. It is the picture of the cross in human form. When we say, "I can't do it any longer," Jesus says, "You don't have to; the battle is already won!" When we provide strength for our brothers and sisters by lifting up their weary arms, we reflect a significant picture of Jesus in their life. "Two are better than one, because they have a good return for their labor: If either of them falls down, one can help the other up. But pity anyone who falls and has no one to help them up" (Ecclesiastes 4:9-10, NIV).

As good teammates, we must remind our community of these biblical promises:

- The battle is won.
- God is for us.
- We're not alone.

- We're more than conquerors.
- Jesus paid it all.
- We don't have to carry this weight by ourselves.

"After the victory, the LORD instructed Moses, 'Write this down on a scroll as a permanent reminder, and read it aloud to Joshua: I will erase the memory of Amalek from under heaven.' Moses built an altar there and named it Yahweh-Nissi (which means 'the LORD is my banner')."

The significance of this moment is bigger than you think. In fact, most times that God would do something paramount for His people, they would build an altar in response and make a monument as a longstanding memorial. This altar moment existed to remind themselves, their community, and the generations that followed that God is faithful and can do it all again as we need Him to. For all of time, Israel has the confidence that the Lord is their banner and their overwhelming force for victory in trial and battle. I believe this moment is important for the community aspect because we experience victory and defeat together.

Our victories affect each other and so do our defeats. Our victories enhance the quality of community we are in; and by proof of this story (and many others), these victories are often experienced because of the quality of community we are in. Therefore, the big question is, do you have these relationships in your life? If not, it's time to forge new relationships and position yourself for victory. I know there are always excuses, and you may lack confidence or feel like there's no one who understands. I get it. I also know that sitting on our hands, complaining, and wishing don't work either.

So, in concluding this chapter, allow me to make a few more specific recommendations for attaining deep community:

Pray for it: My friend William says, "Nothing happens until something is spoken." Approach the heart of God and ask for friendships that improve your life and also those where you can improve the lives of others. Speak it in faith, declare that you are worthy of these relationships, and humbly ask God to give them to you.

Meet needs: The best way to forge new relationships is to find out what people need and then meet it. Nothing bonds us quite like meeting the need of another person, especially when it isn't our "responsibility" to do so.

Repair brokenness: Sometimes new and needed relationships won't appear in your life because you haven't stewarded the previous ones well. If there are relational rifts now coming to mind, a good start would be to make peace with others and sow good seeds once again. You never know; those repaired relationships could be exactly what you needed all along.

Don't be annoying and needy: If you are overwhelming and constantly needy, people will likely keep their distance. This doesn't mean be totally cool and aloof—we all want to be wanted. But relationships are give and take, and each season requires a different grace. If all you are is a taker, then you're not going to be the first on anyone's call list. Check your neediness level and monitor it.

Expand your network: If there are areas in your life where you feel a lid, whether that be financial, career, leadership, or relationships, then this is a good time to do something different to break through that ceiling. Regarding needed relationships, sometimes expanding your network is exactly what you need to find new, strategic relationships that burst you through your lid(s). This is uncomfortable at times but worth the effort. Go find some new people and rub shoulders, or find some new networks and expand. You never know what might come of it.

CHAPTER 10
FRENEMIES

"It's a lot easier to be angry at someone than it is to tell them you're hurt."
-Zakiya Caswell

I saw a post on social media the other day from a man who had a conversation with a stranger on an airplane. He asked the stranger, "Why don't you attend church?" The stranger's answer was not "I don't have time" or "I don't believe in God." On the contrary, his answer was "I don't go to church because everyone there is a hypocrite." My social media friend replied, "Then you can't go to work, school, the playground, or anywhere else for that matter, because we're all hypocrites." The other guy replied, "Ya got me there!"

I can't help but wonder why this man's church experience was so poor that he'd given up on it completely. It makes me sad, because my overall church experiences have been full of excitement, wonderful friendships, and fulfillment. I'm also not so naive as to think that there aren't some bad churches out there doing more harm than good. Even still, to give up on church completely? What would this guy's life be like had he voiced that hurt and worked toward reconciliation? When you remove yourself over an offense, you steal the opportunity from the people on the other side of that offense to grow and get better. Your difficult experience might turn into a greater blessing to your community if handled appropriately.

Now, I don't know this man's specific situation, and it doesn't make a ton of sense to speculate. According to research from Tel Aviv University and the Massachusetts Institute of Technology, we have poor perception in assessing who our friends are, meaning that only half of our friends actually consider themselves our friends.[25] My initial reaction is that this can't be true. Half? Seriously? It does make me think that we are really good at romanticizing relationships. For instance, in a romantic setting, you go on one good date and you've planned the wedding by the time you've brushed your teeth for bed. In the meantime, the other person isn't even sure they want to go on another date with you. You know you've done it!

As humans, we're really good at assuming the best or worst of others and exaggerating the truth to make ourselves feel better. If not careful, we can also manipulate a situation to selfishly position ourselves for a better outcome. This is, sadly, simply human nature. These tendencies create unintended splits in the fabric of relationships we need or desire the most. The reality is, we are going to make mistakes in relationships and fail one another. This is to be expected, but we also can't use our human frailty as an excuse to (excuse my language) screw each other over.

There are two kinds of people in relationships: those who take advantage and hurt purposely, and those who make honest

---

25. American Friends of Tel Aviv University, "We are bad judges of friendship, new study shows: Researchers find inability to determine who our real friends are limits our powers of persuasion," ScienceDaily, May 5, 2016.

mistakes and cause hurt unintentionally. In that same vein, there are a few different ways of responding when we mess up, and I'll list a few I've noticed most frequently. Before I do, note that all of these personality traits cause relational cracks that desperately need to be sealed, otherwise they will lead to unintended "frenemies."

I'm giving you these five personalities below as a litmus test to see if you can recognize any of these unhealthy characteristics in your relationships and in your own personal responses. As you do, it might help you track why some of your relationships are broken. Here we go:

> *The Avoider:* You get embarrassed after making a mistake and try to avoid the consequences of it. If you really were honest with yourself, there might be a mountain of problems under a rug somewhere in your soul. The dust bunnies are collecting and your relationships are cracking.

> *The Denier:* You've been caught or found out but won't admit to any wrongdoing. This leads to a distorted reality and an inability to determine what is really true after a while.

> *The Blamer:* You're full of excuses, you point lots of fingers, and your whys are always centered around someone else. Pretty soon, your pride causes an odor that keeps people at more than arm's distance.

> *The Fixer:* You try to fix the mistake by covering up your tardiness, forgetfulness, or whatever it may be. The only way

for you to cover it up is to lie and say you've handled it or have it under control when you haven't.

The Manipulator: You are tremendous with words, and while you're willing to assume some blame, you tend to reframe the problem as a greater problem that caused the problem you caused. In other words, it's not your fault, even though it is your fault. You're the victim and the problem you caused is actually the solution. You expect people to now thank you for the pain you've caused. I believe that, when unchecked, this characteristic is very dangerous and the quickest way to level down fast.

Can you identify yourself in any of these? Chances are, if you've been alive for more than a month, you are guilty of one or two. Guess what? So am I. I'm going to say something a bit crazy and I hope it gives you some peace. I actually believe that God very much allows us to be flawed and mistake-prone. He uses and leverages our mistakes for our good and even the good of those we hurt. We just need to be able to see the beauty in the complicated messes that life sometimes makes. *So how do we do that?* I'm so glad you asked. Deflating and de-escalating strife between each other is not only important, it is necessary and a responsibility of the believer. God desires unity in His body and didn't send Jesus to die for our sins so that we could hurt each other with our sin nature. We were made for healthy community that forgives and lives in unity. Before I give solutions and practical steps to repairing relationships and effectively navigating conflict, we're going to need a framework for God's heartbeat regarding unity within healthy relationships.

UNITY > DIVERSITY

As a church, we have some core values that we hope our people will embody as we fulfill our mission of "reviving our city, one block at a time"—hence our name, The Block Church. One of our original values was "diversity." We wanted to be a church that was diverse in age, race, economic status, and idea. Our hope has been that we might foster a place where very different people are able to coexist. We felt this would be pleasing to the Lord, and it has been. Our church is incredibly diverse, with many of the qualities I mentioned above. Before we planted, I envisioned a church where, by the power of God, fifteen-year-olds would offer wisdom to fifty-year-olds, and the wealthy would hold hands with the poor as we all sing songs our church has written. There's definitely proof that God is at work in this way here. Let me tell you two stories that encourage me that He is doing something deep and real.

First, during our pre-launch phase, our team met with a local pastor in the neighborhood we were starting in. He told us we would *never* have a diverse church here because it was too racially divided. Frankly, I was quite dismayed after that conversation because we were out of time and venue ideas. Truthfully, I was about to give up on launching our church after that moment. We had been through a lot and this neighborhood and particular venue were the only ones available after a year on the ground.

There was a couple who was on our launch team who represented that diversity we talked about. Segun was a doctor from Nigeria who grew up in Great Britain. His fiancée, Linda, was a feminist, a liberal, and mixed. I'm kind of traditional to be honest, and probably more conservative than some people may like, especially as we began our church. However, these individuals and many others have taught me so much. As we had honest and mature discussions about the state of the world, the more I listened, the more I learned, and the more ground we covered.

I owe a great deal to Segun and Linda, because they were the ones who stood up and told our team, "This is exactly where we are supposed to plant! This is what the church is supposed to do: break down walls and barriers. Sure, it'll be difficult, but not as hard as the original church." All of us were like, oh yeah, duh! And after that moment, we pressed on, signed our contract, and launched an incredibly diverse church from day one. It was especially a blessing to me, because I grew up in Orlando, Florida, and was surrounded by a large Puerto Rican community in our church. The smell of *pastelillos* after church and the community's loud, boisterous love were some things I had longed for ever since I had moved away from Orlando. The crazy thing is, where our original church location is positioned is very close to the largest Puerto Rican population in Philadelphia. Is God crazy or what? He knows all and is so sovereign.

This second story will touch your heart as well. There's a lady in our church who has lived in the same neighborhood her entire life. She was raised Irish-Catholic in this very prejudiced and, some would even say, racist community where we were going to launch our church. Growing up, she heard her family talk about the blacks or Hispanics crossing over their neighborhood's historic dividing street lines. Racism was ingrained in her by the passing of the baton from one generation to the next, just like so many other sins in our culture. Fast forward a few years, and this lady had been faithful to our church and was experiencing close relationship with God like she had never known in the rigged religion she was raised in. She even invited her daughter and granddaughter, as well as others from the community, to come with her.

I remember one night she came up to me and said (in her Philadelphian accent), "Pasta' Joe, I gotta tell ya a story." She confessed to me that her whole life she had been racist. She had been raised that way and had stuck with it because it was all she knew. But since coming to The Block Church, God had been slowly stripping this negative and ungodly stronghold from her life. She said, "How can I look at [so and so, a black girl] and be racist? She is the most beautiful person I know and is filled with the presence of God. I must repent." Wow, take that, local neighborhood pastor who almost made me quit! Maybe that's a bit petty of me, but I'm so glad that I didn't quit and that Segun and Linda were with us to be used by God in saying this was home.

After a couple years of emphasizing our diversity slogan, people really started to get to know each other through small groups and events. We navigated a very divisive election together, including protests, police shootings, and national anthem protests. You name it, it's been a bizarre and wild time to be a pastor of a diverse community of people. We started to gather together and converse about race and reconciliation. To be honest, I didn't know what any of that meant. I didn't realize that our language of diversity was actually more an inhibitor than a unifier.

What I learned from this is that you can have a diverse church without it being a *unified* church. Diversity is actually easy to accomplish, but it's experiencing *unity* that is the real work. This takes leadership, patience, honesty, tears, losing financial contributors and volunteers who don't like the conversation—basically, it takes some guts. The right things in life are usually difficult but they are always worth it. So, here we are. I believe we have a unified church, with Republicans, Democrats, young, old, poor, wealthy, red, yellow, black, and white. Most important, we have Christ followers who are building their identity on the words of Jesus.

We are not perfect, but we are in a beautiful, complicated process. We celebrate and embrace our diversity. We have conversations that are difficult, and we apologize regularly because we know that *authentic community will be full of "I'm sorry," "Let's try again," and "Please understand."* We've decided that we are not colorblind or afraid to talk about how God has blessed us. Instead, we celebrate our differences while guarding against those differences becoming our identities. We fight to be one, daily. We've chosen *unity* over *diversity*.

WHAT'S UNITY?

And the four living creatures, each of them with six wings, are full of eyes all around and within, and day and night they never cease to say, "Holy, holy, holy, is the Lord God Almighty, who was and is and is to come!" (Revelation 4:8, ESV)

What you just read is a picture of heaven and the heart of God. The Bible describes the four creatures as an ox, a lion, a man, and an eagle—all very different, but very much one as they sing out praises to their King. This is what pleases God. It takes faith to put aside our differences and worship from these differences. Most people who hate those who look different or have different opinions do so simply out of fear. This is pride and certainly not of God.

Unity is when one drops one's privilege and another leaves their disadvantage so that they both can join as one. This statement is a shot from a gun to all things prideful, and if you feel some sort of way about that statement, then that's your pride experiencing a major *ouch*. This is why pursuing unity inevitably leads to conflict. We're all fighting against our pride while embracing the Kingdom and the true essence of love.

Jesus says, "There is no greater love than to lay down one's life for one's friends" (John 15:13, NLT). That's what unity is: laying down your pride for your friends and the greater good and taking up the mission of Jesus. Trust me, the pursuit of unity provides a tension we must manage and keep fighting for. Almost everything in our current culture and media presses us to separate and huddle in our groups. However, everything in scripture presses us to come together even when we disagree or are hurt. There is conflict in every church on the planet, yet *I believe that great churches leverage conflict and dying churches ignore it.* Here are some things to remember:

- Conflicts are going to happen; expect to experience them at some point.
- Conflicts can be sinful, and we have a responsibility to resolve them in a timely manner.
- Conflicts are opportunities, so seize them because God is often using them to unify us.

Here is Jesus' teaching on conflict:

> If another believer sins against you, go privately and point
> out the offense. If the other person listens and confesses it,
> you have won that person back. But if you are unsuccessful,
> take one or two others with you and go back again, so that
> everything you say may be confirmed by two or three wit-
> nesses. If the person still refuses to listen, take your case to
> the church. Then if he or she won't accept the church's deci-
> sion, treat that person as a pagan or a corrupt tax collector.
> (Matthew 18:15-17, NLT)

Christ calls us to confront the conflict and come together in
unity. In the passage above, Jesus gives us four practical steps for
staying unified in the midst of conflict:

1. **Go to those who hurt you and gently point it out.** Many
   of us avoid these situations and allow these feelings to fes-
   ter because we fear conflict. Or we talk about our frustration to anyone but the person who made us frustrated and
   offended. The next thing we know, we've left our faith community, are angry at others for not taking our side even
   though they don't have the full story, and are now set up to
   be offended again. This spirit of offense is rotten, and once
   we allow it to take root in our life, it becomes easier and
   easier to get offended and hurt by ridiculous things. The
   reality is, most people who hurt us made an honest mistake
   and wish they could take it back. They may not even know
   they've hurt us. How could they, unless we tell them? Don't

be passive; be *aggressive* against the sin and address this situation so that you can get the weight off your shoulders.

2. If addressing the problem with the person who offended you doesn't resolve the issue, go back and **take one or two friends with you, not to gossip, but to get an objective point of view**. It could be possible that you are offended unnecessarily and your other friends will help you see that. Maybe your counterpart can't see that they were wrong in the situation and need friends to illuminate their error. You'll never know unless you try, and that's why this is the biblical way. If you recognize that you are the one in the wrong, there's absolutely nothing that heals us quite like an apology. Say you're sorry, and watch freedom and peace walk into the room. In fact, I always counsel people in conflict to apologize if there is even a hint of something they may have done wrong. We have to remove the barrier of pride and learn to lead with "I'm sorry." Why? Because I don't believe anything facilitates unity more than an apology, especially when it isn't our fault.

3. If those two steps don't work, you should now **take it to a church leader**. This could be a volunteer leader, a pastor, an elder, etc. Look for someone from a different peer group (usually older) in a recognized position of authority within your church. Usually, at this point, there is some clear resolution, healing is taking place, and a stronger bond is being built as well. Since you've made such a great effort to honor God and each other, you tend to experience quicker fruit from the situation. In my opinion, honor is the greatest seed we can sow.

4. **If the conflict still remains unresolved after getting your leadership involved, treat them like Jesus treated tax collectors** (that's what He says to do), who were the worst of the worst in biblical times. I ponder this scripture often, and I of course understand that there are some cultural differences between then and now. I do think about how Jesus treated these individuals and my solution is different from what you might expect. Jesus called Matthew, a tax collector (and the author here), to follow Him. Jesus dined with Zacchaeus, also a tax collector. He healed pagans, forgave sinners, and fed the outcasts. The point I'm making is that when someone breaks your heart, you might need to distance yourself from them for a season (after attempting to deal with the issue). You have permission. You're still called to love them, pray for them, and believe for reconciliation. You are still purposed for unity, no matter how harmful the conflict. When someone refuses to acknowledge you anymore, or is slandering you, remember that you're in good company. Jesus was mocked, betrayed, and murdered by His own people. One moment, they were shouting praises; the next, they were shouting curses. Life is fickle and so are people, but *you don't have to be*. Fight for unity.

In the midst of all this, Paul the apostle tells us in Acts to strive always to keep our consciences clear before God and man (see Acts 24:16). He says in Romans to do all we can to live at peace with God and man (see Romans 12:18). Again in Romans, he pleads that we should make every effort to do whatever leads to peace (see Romans 14:19). Finally, in Ephesians, he asks that we make every effort to keep the unity of the spirit (see Ephesians 4:3).

If you want unity, it will undoubtedly come with work and discomfort. Unity is, without question, a call to maturity and responsibility. Can I help you mature? I'll close this chapter with one final soapbox. Have you heard of the term "ghosting"? It's a word the kids came up with for when you don't text someone back or when you disappear from a relationship without explanation. Nothing makes me crazier than ghosting. It's my mission to work this out of our people and out of the body of Christ. There is nothing more disrespectful, dishonoring, and immature than to disappear because you don't like something that was said or done. Talk about causing disunity!

Our proper response should always be one of grace. If you don't like what someone says, let them know in a careful and gentle way. I get it, we can't and shouldn't respond to everything; and sometimes we need a little space to process our answer. Why not tell them that instead of just falling off the face of the planet? A simple "I'll get back to you" isn't going to kill you, and it will help them. I've noticed this epidemic with church volunteers who are tired and burned out but who won't communicate that to leaders. They then disappear, leaving their team high and dry. I've noticed it in stories of friends who texted something they shouldn't and don't hear from the other person for months.

I can go on and on with examples, but my desperate plea is for us to work toward unity. We do this by *not* ghosting people. There's no way someone can apologize to you if they don't know they've hurt you. There's also no way for you to grow if you run from an uncomfortable situation. I'm saddened that technology is at the root of this; it can do so much good, but it also affords us the opportunity to cause much hurt. I beg of you: don't get in the habit of sending long, angry text messages or no messages at all. Man up, woman up, level up, and have conversations face to face. We owe it to each other. We are brothers and sisters in Christ and sons and daughters of one Father. How can we please Him and reap great relational fruit in our lives? We do it His way and continually work toward unity.

CHAPTER 11

FRIENDLY FIRE

"Integrity is telling myself the truth. And honesty is telling the truth to other people."
-Spencer Johnson

Have you ever heard the phrase "love is war"? Well, it's kind of true. Anything in life worth its salt is worth fighting for. Sadly, many people unintentionally fight against those they are supposed to be fighting for, which can lead to friendly fire and relational loss. The psalmist writes in Psalm 27:3, "Though a mighty army surrounds me, my heart will not be afraid" (NLT). While he could be referring to a variety of things, the truth is that our heart is at war. It is in a fight for godliness and a search for real truth.

God proved our purpose for healthy human connection in the garden by creating two humans who needed each other. As their hearts battled against the serpent (aka Satan, who is a liar, thief, and deceiver of the heart), they lost significantly—as will you if you're not equipped to fight. Humans were designed for connection, but if we aren't vigilant in guarding our hearts, this interdependence can get very skewed, causing heart trauma and debilitating anxieties.

The heart is a funny and confusing thing. I wrote about this earlier in this book but I feel highly compelled to elaborate on its function more thoroughly in this chapter. For us to go higher, we have to dig deeper, and the heart is the deepest place we can search. Now, we often hear "guard your heart," "follow your heart," "check your heart," or even "what's your heart saying?" Some of this is ambiguous and perplexing. These statements are actually a bit mythical and could be a dangerous thing to say without proper understanding of the heart's function. I've thought to myself before, *Does my heart that is pumping blood speak? Why is the heart connected to romance and emotion?* It's kind of mysterious if you think about it.

According to an article in *Today*, there have been studies conducted on how the heart and the brain interact when it comes to emotions. According to a 2006 study, our hearts and our brains are constantly talking—and more often than not, it's our heart talking over our brain. With a direct line to the brain, our hearts have a huge amount of control over the rest of our body. "As we experience feelings like anger, frustration, anxiety and insecurity, our heart rhythm patterns become more erratic. These erratic patterns are sent to the emotional centers in the brain, which it recognizes as negative or stressful feelings. These signals create the actual feelings we experience in the heart area and the body. The erratic heart rhythms also block our ability to think clearly."[26]

Now I don't necessarily want to get into the history of the heart as a metaphor, but I do want us to understand how managing the metaphor of the heart plays a big factor in having appropriate

26. "Does Your Heart Sense Your Emotional State?" *Today*, October 14, 2016. www.today.com/health/does-your-heart-sense-your-emotional-state-2D80555354.

boundaries, clarity in relationships, and equally strong integrity. Why? Because the heart and emotions are absolutely connected. When we say we're following our heart, we are often following our emotions, and those emotions can get us into major trouble. Several passages in the Bible refer to the heart. Here are a few examples: "trust in the Lord with all of your heart" (Proverbs 3:5); "take delight in the Lord and He will give you your heart's desires" (Psalm 37:4); "create in me a clean heart" (Psalm 51:10); "I will praise You, Lord my God, with all my heart" (Psalm 86:12); and "don't let your hearts be troubled" (John 14:1).

What does this all mean? I believe the authors are referring to the power of the incredible emotion connected metaphorically to the heart. That said, the scriptures lead us to understand that worshiping and relationally conversing with God happen via the mind, body, and soul. Ultimately, the heart encompasses all of those items combined into one function; so, to say that the heart *only* functions based on emotion would be wrong. No, it's way more scientific and spiritual than that. The heart directs our thoughts and words, its welfare affects our body, and it is the gateway to our soul. On the other hand, what we say and think can damage the heart; what we put into our bodies can literally kill the heart; and what we do with our time, talent, and treasure postures the heart to either build the soul or destroy it. So, to say that the heart is just a "thing" would be a great understatement.

HEART TRANSPLANT

From 1987 to June 2016, survival rates following pediatric heart transplantation at Monroe Carell Jr. Children's Hospital at

Vanderbilt were the following: 94 percent at one month, 89 percent at one year, 77 percent at five years, and 72 percent at 10 years.[27] In other words, the survival rate of a heart transplant is pretty good. Why does that matter? The scriptures certainly tell us we need a new heart:

> The human heart is the most deceitful of all things, and desperately wicked. Who really knows how bad it is? (Jeremiah 17:9, NLT)

We need to come to Jesus like children for a statistically proven "spiritual pediatric heart transplant." We call this regeneration. Titus explains:

> He saved us, not because of works done by us in righteousness, but according to his own mercy, by the washing of regeneration and renewal of the Holy Spirit, whom he poured out on us richly through Jesus Christ our Savior. (Titus 3:5-6, ESV)

Basically, God is trying to hook us up with a new heart that allows us to most effectively conquer life and have healthy relationships with people. John Piper says, "New birth is the cause of faith, but loving people is the fruit of faith."[28]

Ask Him to take this heart of stone and turn it into a heart of flesh, as referred to in the book of Ezekiel. If you make this

27. "Heart Transplant Survival Rates and Risks," Monroe Carell Jr. Children's Hospital at Vanderbilt. www.childrenshospital.vanderbilt.org/services.php?mid=4604.
28. John Piper, "Regeneration, Faith, Love: In that Order," *Desiring God*. www.desiring-god.org/messages/regeneration-faith-love-in-that-order.

declaration and follow it by surrendering your time, talent, and treasure, I am completely convinced your life will change forever. By the way, getting some godly people around you, plugging into a healthy local church, and slowly reading through the scriptures will make a huge difference on your journey. You don't have to be perfect; just be honest. God is way more into honesty than hypocrisy.

CHECK YOUR HEART

Christian comedian John Crist has a comedy bit and even has a T-shirt that says "Check your heart." He is suggesting that we check our motives and emotions, otherwise we could get caught up in unnecessary drama. Some of you are like, "I love drama!" But for the rest of us who want to live effective lives, we're trying to limit pain in relationships and stay away from personal headaches. Who has time for that? Probably only the people who aren't focusing on important things. I'm trying to help you understand that while we can trust our regenerated heart, we also have to manage our emotions and constantly guard what goes into our mind, body, and soul. We are easily susceptible to *serving* our emotions rather than *managing* them, and there's a significantly large difference between the two. When we serve our emotions, our tendencies decide what we do, where we go, and who we become. When we manage our emotions, our principles guide our decision making. We must be people who manage our emotions so that we can serve others and guard our time, talents, and treasures best. Look what Peter tells us:

> But you are a chosen people, a royal priesthood, a holy nation, God's special possession, that you may declare the praises of him who called you out of darkness into his wonderful light. (1 Peter 2:9, NLT)

This scripture reminds me that my existence is predicated on my declarations. I am the things above so that I may declare this truth: I'm a Christ follower! This notion dictates how I live, the decisions I make, the places I go, how and what I do. Why? Because my identity is in *whose* I am, not in *what* I do.

YES OR NO

If you don't read the Bible, you're really missing out. Jesus was honestly a savage. The things He would say can be both hilarious and sometimes disturbing (particularly if you don't study the context or language). One time, He told a crowd to eat His flesh and drink His blood. Most were out after that. Of course, there was meaning in the metaphor, but it was tough for some to hang on to find out what it really meant. I love and wrestle with what Jesus says in Matthew 5:37: "Just say a simple, 'Yes, I will,' or 'No, I won't.' Anything beyond this is from the evil one" (NLT).

A few verses earlier, Jesus is tackling murder, adultery, and other hot topics. Here, He switches gears and goes right for the heart, both literally and figuratively. I very much believe that at the core of Christianity is an underlying notion that Jesus followers, while accepted as imperfect people, are still striving to be incredibly trustworthy and full of integrity. The nucleus of the Christian faith should be that people can put their trust and hope in us because we carry good news and serve a holy God. So, if that's the case, we must improve on some of the new stereotypes of Christianity (e.g., bad tippers, liars when singing worship songs, gossipers, late, etc.). What do people stereotype you as?

I believe the reason so many of us get into relational trouble is that we have an integrity problem. Maybe we've slid into someone's DMs who we simply shouldn't have. Maybe we promised to go somewhere with someone but backed out last minute because we never meant to go in the first place or it wasn't convenient in that moment. Maybe we talk trash online or through text messages but avoid conflict in person. I'm not trying to make you feel bad, but I am attempting to shine a light on areas where we unintentionally create relational chaos for ourselves.

FIRST-WORLD PROBS

My brother-in-law lives on a mountain top in a beautiful Philadelphia suburb. He has major views and a stunning home. I often spend time there during the holidays, and he will complain to me with a smirk on his face about all the leaves he has to clean up and the wood he has to gather for his cozy fireplace. He then jokingly says, "I know, I know, Valley Forge probs." We laugh and then I help him. Okay, maybe I only helped once. But the point I'm making is that we live in a world where convenience and comfort have both enhanced and distanced relationships.

I recently listened to a Pastor Craig Groeschel sermon in which he listed the stats below about phone usage. He started with the word "nomophobia." "Nomophobia" is defined as the irrational fear of being without your mobile phone or being unable to use your phone for some reason, such as the absence of a signal or running out of data or battery power. He went on to list that 77 percent of 18- to 24-year-olds won't hand you their phone, and 58 percent of people don't go one waking hour without checking their phone. He said that 59 percent of people check their email as it comes in and 89 percent check it daily on vacation. Geez. Additionally, 80 percent of teenagers sleep with their phones, and 84 percent of people believe they couldn't go one day without their phones. We're addicted! The challenge with this, as you know, is that we can cancel on people last minute. Back in the day, if we made a date or put something in our written calendar, we'd have to follow through with our commitment because it would be impossible to send a last-minute text message backing out so that we could do something "better" that we saw on Instagram earlier.[29]

These are our first-world, new-world problems and we have to find a way to overcome them. Here are a few ways we can start: lowering our weapon, defining relationships, not using technology as an excuse, making the right decisions, honoring boundaries, and evaluating our motives.

LOWER OUR WEAPON

I titled this chapter "Friendly Fire" because unless we have integrity and are honest with each other, we will end up hurt and could potentially damage our relationships beyond repair.

29. Craig Goeschel, "#Struggles," Elevation Church, October 25, 2015. elevationchurch. org/sermons/struggles/.

Honesty can undoubtedly be complicated sometimes, but dishonesty usually comes back to bite us later. Therefore, the best way to stop hurting each other is to lower our weapons, wave our white flags, look each other in the eye, and deal. In closing, I've included some detailed advice on how to effectively lower your weapon and stop coming for your friends.

DEFINE RELATIONSHIPS

Most of the time, those who have bad intentions, or who don't know what they want, will stay ambiguous and lead others along for too long. This chapter is about friendship, but sometimes friendship lines get crossed. Sometimes we're not sure where we stand in a relationship because we've kissed or been physical. I highly recommend defining what you are at different benchmarks of your relational journey. If a friendship turns into something more, it's okay to simply acknowledge it. Don't lie and say you're just friends when you're cuddling on the couch while watching a movie. Just own it.

I particularly find it frustrating when lonely individuals take advantage of those who they know like them romantically. You may find yourself sending or receiving a message on a social app that suggests the potential for being more than friends when you have no interest in that type of relationship with that person. If these things continue to happen without definition, then this is problematic and can lead to hurt. Don't enable someone to do this to you and don't use someone else whom you have no intention of getting to know.

There are some of us who need specific acquaintances or relationships for specific seasons. I also don't think this is wrong, but it can be hard. I do have to acknowledge that, as a pastor, this theme rises up often. Some get frustrated when certain relationships are seasonal or difficult to maintain. Again, I highly recommend and personally practice over-communication. We owe others that extension of grace so that they can manage their expectations with us.

STOP USING TECHNOLOGY AS AN EXCUSE

How often do we lie and say, "I didn't get your message" or "I missed your call" or "My number changed/I got a new phone"? Of course, those things happen, but we lean on these excuses too much. People are God's economy and human interaction is the greatest gift we've been given. Let's stop canceling because it's convenient or being late because we know we can just text someone an apology. Let's stop being rude over text message and blaming it on the way it was read. Technology is a gift. Let's not use it as a weapon.

MAKE RIGHT DECISIONS

Having integrity and leveraging our new heart is all about making the *right* decisions, not just the decisions that *feel* right. Sometimes we don't feel like doing it, but that's usually how we know it's the right thing to do. People of God, people of character, people of integrity: let's make hard decisions and get comfortable with that tension. As we do, the fruit of God's blessing will follow. Remember, we exist to declare the glory of God, and our thoughts, decisions, and feet follow our new heart, not our bubbling emotions.

DEVELOP BOUNDARIES

The word "no" can be a healthy person's best friend. While friendship sometimes carries the responsibility to inconvenience ourselves for others, we also have a responsibility to sometimes say no to guard ourselves. The best and healthiest version of us makes for a much better world, and often that starts with creating boundaries. If you keep getting taken advantage of, practice saying no, even when you're afraid. For instance, if you've been out every night of the week spending money you don't have and you haven't spent any time with God, then you might have a boundary problem. Dr. Henry Cloud and Dr. John Townsend wrote a book called *Boundaries* that has sold over one million copies. The tagline is "When to Say Yes, How to Say No to Take Control of Your Life." Now's the time to take control of your life!

CONTINUALLY EVALUATE YOUR MOTIVES

Finally, we must evaluate the motives of our heart regularly. The Bible tells us to examine ourselves and take an inventory of our thoughts, emotions, and direction. When making decisions about our relationships, we should invite the Holy Spirit to lead. "Holy Spirit, what are You saying and how are You leading?" is always a safe prayer to pray under your breath. It's easy to selfishly manipulate people or situations, but the best way for us to guard against that is by inviting God into our moment-by-moment existence.

Often, I find myself praying the same statement as John: "He must become greater and greater, and I must become less and less" (John 3:30, NLT). I also recommend praying what Jesus prayed as

He faced imminent death: "Yet I want your will to be done, not mine" (Luke 22:42b, NLT).

WOULD YOU PRAY WITH ME?

Pretty intense chapter? It was for me too. As I write this, I definitely sense areas of conviction in which I can make changes. How about you? I'd like to close this portion of our reading with a prayer and I invite you to pray along with me:

Jesus, we need You in every aspect of our relationships. We offer You our hearts. Please wash them by Your Word and voice and help us produce fruit that pleases You by serving others. We want to be better friends and to have more integrity in our approach to life. We give You permission to convict us when we are unhealthy, when we take advantage of others, and when we make decisions based on emotions alone. We make decisions based on Your lordship and we love You because You lead us best. Thank You for leading us from love as You first loved us. Guard us from offense and bitterness in all things. Right now, we give all of our current and future relationships to You. In Jesus' name we pray, amen.

PART 4

AUTHORITY AND INSTITUTIONS

CHAPTER 12

TRUST ISSUES

**"Oh oh, trust issues
Oh oh, trust issues
Oh oh, trust issues"
-Drake**

It was a steaming-hot summer night, and church had just ended. I had just preached my fourth sermon of the day and was completely exhausted. Sweat was pouring down my head and back as I held my adorable son (who is not light by any means) and half-heartedly greeted people as they exited our sixth service of the day. Don't get me wrong: most weeks I really like to high five and hug people, because I genuinely love them. In fact, since the beginning of our church, I have always committed myself to greeting people after service. I don't know why I feel like I need to do it. Maybe it's because I noticed my pastor doing it when I was growing up. Maybe it's my own insecurity that, if the churchgoers don't have a personal touch with their pastor, they won't come back. Maybe I like to hear feedback from a good sermon or one I'm not sure was so good. Maybe it's because I like to observe our volunteers in their roles and to connect with new people. Maybe it's because I like to keep my ear to the ground to keep track of how the experience was. Maybe it's a combination of all of these things.

Whatever the reason, I do it as much as I can. And on this night, I struck up a conversation with a girl who let it all out, right there on the curb. My typical question to someone I don't recognize is "How was your experience, and how many times have you been here?" The girl replied, "This is my second time. I came many months ago. It was really good, and I liked your talking or whatever you do up there because it makes me feel emotional and also uncomfortable." Of course, I knew the interpretation. "I liked your talking" equals "You made me laugh," and "It makes me feel emotional" equals "The Holy Spirit was moving on my heart and I can't quite explain what happened." "It makes me feel uncomfortable" equals "There are things in my life that you somehow knew about while you were talking." Sometimes people go on to ask me, "How did you know? There are some changes I need to make, and this sermon reminded me of all those things. Did my friend tell you?" Meanwhile, I'm thinking to myself, *No, that's just the point of preaching!* I said to this girl, "Thanks, I know what you mean," and then asked her why it had been so long since she'd been back. She told me, "It isn't you; it's this whole church thing in general. I don't fully understand it, and mainly I've just got real trust issues."

MISSING OUT

Jeffry A. Simpson wrote, "Trust involves the juxtaposition of people's loftiest hopes and aspirations with their deepest worries and fears." This description makes it clear why so many people have trouble trusting. For them, the benefits of closeness and intimacy are overshadowed by the possibility of pain and betrayal.[30] These issues play out in our lives in a variety of ways, and listed below are a few possible examples of how our trust issues can manifest:

- We might be skeptical of anyone in authority without even giving them an opportunity.
- We could be making everyone prove themselves to us.
- We might be taking our anger out on someone who didn't do anything wrong because we're still upset at the person before them.
- We might intentionally look for or try to catch someone in a lie.
- We might try to predict how others will betray us and those we love.
- We might mistake small blunders for major breaches of trust.
- We could be rude or standoffish to someone who we actually desire to connect with (whether that be a friendship, mentorship, romantic relationship, etc.).
- We could be looking for issues with a person or organization instead of acknowledging all the potentials and good qualities of those people and institutions.
- We could be totally lacking in joy, fun, and happiness due to our trust issues and not even realize it.
- We might find ourselves very alone, insecure, isolated, angry, and going backward in our careers.

30. Rita Watson, "Oxytocin: The Love and Trust Hormone Can Be Deceptive," *Psychology Today* (Sussex Publishers), October 14, 2014. www.psychologytoday.com/us/blog/love-and-gratitude/201310/oxytocin-the-love-and-trust-hormone-can-be-deceptive.

- We could be missing out on greater opportunities, but our unwillingness to trust is limiting our potential in all facets of life.

In my opinion, *it would be sad to miss out on life's best because of someone else's worst.* But we do it all the time out of the overwhelming fear of being let down. Many people who carry these trust issues (maybe even you) can backtrack the root of the problem to being let down by someone close to them in a big way. The psychologist Erik Erikson says (my paraphrase) that the initial trust of a child is built during infancy as an adult consistently meets its needs and, by the end of year one, trust is established. Psychoanalyst/pediatrician D. W. Winnicott believed that predictability on the part of parents was critical to building trust in their baby. In his book *Talking to Parents,* he wrote, "Parents, and especially the mother at the start, are taking a lot of trouble to shield the child from that which is unpredictable."[31] In other words, when those we expect to be most consistent with us are not, it creates internal insecurities that bleed into other areas in our lives.

No doubt a parent, significant other, or sibling may have hurt you, which in turn led you to complicated trust challenges. But for this particular chapter, I want to focus on individuals whom we see as authority figures or mentors in our lives. Since trust is established so early on in those types of relationships, those wounds have the potential to be the deepest. We expect those leading us to keep us safe, and when that doesn't happen, it breaks us.

---

31. Joyce Catlett, "Trust Issues: Why Is It So Hard for Some People to Trust?" PsychAlive, September 25, 2017. www.psychalive.org/trust-issues/.

For a moment, imagine a parent being absent most of your life, a teacher or babysitter crossing the line, a spiritual leader who broke your spirit or had a failure themselves. These instances leave us broken, lost, and with more questions than a lifetime of therapy could answer. The list of let-downs can go on and on, and each situation is different, but the situation is likely this: somewhere along the way, we got hurt by an authority figure or figures, and now skepticism has become our religion. Those who have been hurt badly by someone they looked up to often find comfort in their new doubts and don't know what steps to take to achieve success in new relationships. The sharp pain, shame, and humiliation of the past become familiar, and these feelings, although quite vexatious, are hard to let go of because we aren't sure how to feel anything else. When not dealt with, this can facilitate a controlling spirit that leads to major complications in future relationships.

START AT THE TOP

According to a *Harvard Business Review* article by Robert Hurley, roughly half of all managers don't trust their leaders. The statistics Hurley quotes are bleak: 69 percent of responses to a 2002 survey agreed with the statement "I just don't know who to trust anymore." A University of Chicago survey of 800 Americans revealed that more than four out of five had "only some" or "hardly any" confidence in the people running major corporations.[32]

That's truly a shame but is, unfortunately, the world we live in. Why is this the case? Well, you probably know the famous John

---

32. Robert F. Hurley, "The Decision to Trust," *Harvard Business Review*, August 21, 2014. hbr.org/2006/09/the-decision-to-trust.

Maxwell quote "Everything rises and falls on leadership."[33] It really is so true in every arena of life. Leaders have the ability to make everything and everyone around them better. Unfortunately, when those in authority aren't good leaders, it often makes everything and everyone around them worse and the atmosphere uproarious. For us to experience healing and triumph in our ability to trust others, it has to start with addressing these issues with authority figures who failed us. I would also say that it is the responsibility of all leaders everywhere to remember that we lead God's people. We steward people just like we steward companies, resources, homes, and material things. In fact, people require much more delicate care.

Toward the end of this chapter, I'll address leaders more specifically, but for now, what are some practical steps we can take to restore our trust issues?

THE F WORD

Get ready, let's say it together. One . . . two . . . three—*I forgive you!* Yep. I believe forgiving the leader who failed you is the key to dealing with your trust issues. I hate to break it to you, but it's the best way. Sure, you can be nicer and speak more positively about them. You can serve them better, work harder, or strike up meaningful conversations that might foster a deeper relationship. However, the real starting point for true healing is through forgiveness. It's God's process and how He designed human reconciliation.

Forgiveness is defined as the act of pardoning an offender. Primarily, forgiveness is accepting that someone failed you and

---

33. John Maxwell, *The 21 Indispensable Qualities of a Leader* (Nashville, TN: Thomas Nelson, Inc., 2007), n.p.

letting them out of the jail you've built in your heart and mind. This is shocking language, I know. To give us a biblical context, the Greek word in the scriptures for "forgiveness" literally means "to let go," as when a person does not demand payment for a debt. Are you getting it by now? If not, take a look at this story from Jesus in the book of Matthew:

> Therefore, the kingdom of heaven is like a king who wanted to settle accounts with his servants. As he began the settlement, a man who owed him ten thousand bags of gold was brought to him. Since he was not able to pay, the master ordered that he and his wife and his children and all that he had be sold to repay the debt. At this the servant fell on his knees before him. "Be patient with me," he begged, "and I will pay back everything." The servant's master took pity on him, canceled the debt and let him go. (Matthew 18:23-27, NIV)

I love how clear-cut this story is. In fact, this passage reveals a few things about forgiveness that should really help us. For instance, forgiveness was designed by God in heaven for humans on Earth, and when we practice forgiveness, we are acting the most like Jesus. Why? Because forgiveness is a clear practice of patience (see 2 Peter 3:9), an obvious act of mercy (see 1 Timothy 1:16), a humbling of the soul (see Philippians 2:8), the greatest example of compassion (see Matthew 9:36), and a chance to love your enemies (see Luke 6:35).

Forgiveness is also accepting the truth while dismissing the wrong. That's why I like this Bible story so much: because of the honesty and reality of the situation, both parties understood it and were ready to face the consequences. I don't believe complete forgiveness can happen without factual information and honest truth coming forth, especially if the offended knows there's pertinent information being withheld—key word: "pertinent." We don't have to share it all, but we must share what's suitable for peace and healing.

Last, forgiveness is releasing the offender without holding any control over their future. We truly forgive others when we let go of resentment and give up any claim to be compensated for the hurt or loss we have suffered. The Bible teaches that unselfish love is the basis for true forgiveness since love does not keep a record of injury, regardless of whether the other person is sorry or not.

For clarity, God is not asking you to be best friends with those who did you wrong. He's asking you to let it go, because He did. We did the same thing to Him and don't deserve to be forgiven, but He still died on the cross for us. At the end of the day, forgiveness is a starting point for your healing. Forgiving someone shows that you trust God and His order, and may I remind you that it is necessary for all believers. Your hurt is not bigger than God's power to heal, and healing takes place when we do things His way.

When forgiving others, here are a few practical ways to begin the process:

Look inward. You're not perfect, and it's possible that you've made a few mistakes in your day as well. When we look at ourselves, it helps us to have grace with one other. If you have bitterness or trust issues, I highly recommend taking time to self-reflect and observe your own patterns, behaviors, and pre-conceived notions about those in authority over you. Ask God if you've missed the mark in your relationships with your su-periors or if you owe any of them an apology. Sometimes we may be unknowing contributors to a wrongdoing, but even so, it is still wise to look inward and ask for our souls to be still and ears to be open to the truth of God in each matter.

Stop obsessing over why. When people (especially those in authority) hurt us, we tend to play the incident over and over again in our head and heart. While getting clarity on what exactly happened is important, obsessing over why it happened doesn't fix anything. In fact, obsessing keeps us from being able to forgive the debtor. Sometimes there is no good reason why certain things happen, which is why closure is often going to be up to us, not others.

Give a clean slate to them and others. You know you've truly forgiven someone when the next person isn't paying for what the previous person did. I realize I've mentioned this several times in this book, but it tends to happen a lot when we have trust issues. Pain certainly makes giving sec-ond chances complicated, but expecting something out of others that you aren't willing to give is distinctly hypocriti-cal and eventually comes back to haunt you. A great way to practice embracing trust is to start over with yourself and give opportunities to others without expecting them to fail you. Speak life over them, believe in them, and put yourself in a position of vulnerability.

Just do it. I have a friend who has struggled most of his adult life with drug addiction. He goes through seasons and phases of incredible sobriety and then, seemingly out of nowhere, relapses. We're talking an entire year of completed step work, then a disappointment or an unexpected situation presents itself and off he goes. There are a lot of factors here, but one of the elements that I believe affects his ability to prosper consistently is his unwillingness to forgive himself and his mom. Growing up, my friend's mom was problematic and inconsistent. She had a drug problem as well and never created a safe and secure environment for him and his siblings. My friend had a son later in life, and in light of his addiction issues, gave up his parental rights. Because of this, he keeps ending up at a place of disappointment with authority, fear of abandonment, and substance abuse that continue to wreak havoc on every relationship in his life. While he is greatly loved and supported and I believe he is so close to overcoming fully without any future relapses, this final stage of his conquest is connected to forgiveness. Many times I have recommended that he do whatever it takes to forgive his mom and reconcile with his son.

As for you, I plead with you to take steps toward forgiveness. Write down the prayers you need to pray and take whatever steps you need to forgive and trust again. I promise that the consequences of unforgiveness are far more damaging than the healing results of letting go.

LEADERS' RESPONSIBILITY

There is a guy in our church who has been attending off and on for nearly two years. We have had multiple counseling sessions throughout this time regarding his dating situation, sleep problems, stress, issues with his parents, and his future. He was dating a girl who didn't have a relationship with God and that continual tension created much unnecessary stress in his life. Each time we met, the misery of toeing the line of being all in with God or all in with his girlfriend kept coming to a head. They eventually broke up (in my opinion, by the grace of God) and he hit his lowest point. One evening, Lauren and I were driving home for the night and he suddenly came to mind. I felt like I was supposed to call him, and I'm thankful I did, as he needed someone badly. So, we turned around, grabbed ice cream, and showed up at his home for an extensive time of prayer and healing. His words were, "Okay, I give in. What steps should I take?" I didn't want to tell him what to do, but over the past couple of years, I had been asking him what he felt God wanted him to do, and it was a process getting to that point. Once he finally asked me for help, we came up with four specific steps for him to take and he fully committed to trying them for one year. I'm a preacher, so I put a "y" at the end of each for some rhythm.

1. Community—Make friends, specifically godly ones.
2. Christianity—Dive into your spirituality and the local church.
3. Therapy—Deal with the deeper issues in your life and past so that you can heal.
4. Accountability—None of the previous steps will work without the right people holding you accountable to this.

Throughout the year, he went all in and really kicked tail. He started off with a 21-day fast and began the four steps we agreed upon. Since then, he's seen 30 specific miracles and answered prayers in his life and family, one of them being a completely redeemed relationship with his father. As he experienced total forgiveness in this area, his sleep apnea was also healed. Wow. God is so faithful.

Here's where I'm going with this. When counseling someone, I try not to tell them what to do but rather point them to scripture to find answers to their questions. I want people to hear from God for themselves and my job is to guide and direct, not dictate. Making decisions for others is often how leaders get in trouble and receive blame. Individuals accuse us when their situations don't work out the way they hoped, and, when hurt, they condemn those who told them what to do. The strategy of helping people decide things for themselves instead of us deciding for them is so much better. By doing this, we've equipped them to need us less and less and lean on God more and more. While leaders are definitely counselors, we are also consultants helping those we love to come to their own God conclusions. We also cannot get into the habit of influencing people for our own gain. They can smell that from a mile away.

Please believe me: there is no possible way to shepherd a large flock, corporation, or organization if everyone is dependent on us alone, and that isn't how God intended it to be. If people are overly dependent on their leaders, those leaders become the substitute for God and will burn out quickly from the amount of care each person requires. As for church leaders, Paul tells us to equip those in our flock for the work of the church (see Ephesians 4:12).

We should sweat over the administrative and equipping aspects and release the ministry to our congregation. As leaders in general, our job is to share our work and bring others along on the journey. The best thing we can do for people is to give them a place to be who God has called them to be and allow them to come to spiritual decisions on their own. Influencing, yes. Ordering, no.

TRUTH, LOVE, AND AUTHENTICITY

What does this have to do with trust? Leaders have a responsibility to be a safe place for those who follow us, submit to us, work for us, and counsel with us. People are the greatest asset and resource we will ever be given. There's no amount of money, property, or gifts that will equal the value of a human life. Because of this, I believe that until we treat people with the same respect and honesty that we ourselves desire, the epidemic of disconnect and mistrust will prevail. We have to do better, and the solution is honesty and authenticity.

I am not getting into a theological discussion on homosexuality in this book, but I do want to tell a brief story about practicing true stewardship of people in a way that's pleasing to God and effective in today's day and age. For a couple of years, there's been a middle-aged man attending our church who is married to another man. This is pretty normal, particularly in a northeastern city and post-Christian culture. But this man is quite different and resilient. For many years, he hopped from church to church searching for an "openly affirming" one that both supported his marriage and illuminated the glories of scripture. He was about to give up when one Sunday, he walked into our church and melted at the presence of God, the Spirit-led preaching, and the authenticity of our community. He eventually got a meeting with me and shared his "situation," fully expecting to be turned away or pushed out. As he fearfully trembled in his communication, I apologized and eased his concerns, assuring him that this was the church of Jesus Christ where we glide on the wings of truth and grace. For months, he and I read books (particularly *People to Be Loved* by Preston Sprinkle) together and dove into the scriptures. We cried, prayed, laughed, respectfully debated, and came to different conclusions.

At our church, we have a policy around leadership and employment that would limit him from taking further steps, but he could serve, be adopted into our community (our form of membership), and even be baptized in water. Again, I don't want to dive into the theology around this here (I can possibly address that via email or in another book), but what I'm leading up to with this story is a phone call we had before his baptism and adoption into our community. On this call, his location pastor and I shared once again our position on homosexuality and what we see as scriptural standard. We reminded him the limits of leadership and brought clarity around baptism being a public commitment to following Jesus. I shared my clear hopes for him and his sexuality, along with my love for him.

His response really surprised me. He said that so many Christian churches bait and switch homosexuals, and from the start we didn't do that. We didn't even shy away from the issue. He loved my sermon series "Sex with the Light On," in which I addressed homosexuality, and he said I shared with incredible grace what I saw as truth. He felt that he could trust us and our church more than any other (including any affirming church) he'd ever been to. He said, "You make me feel like an equal human, and nothing is more meaningful." He went on to share that he is going to continue to wrestle with this particular issue and keep seeking the scriptures and Jesus on it for the rest of his life. He promised that I'd be the first to know if he comes to another conclusion.

Ultimately, leaders, we are helping our people take next steps on their journey with God. Leadership isn't about us or what we're building, but rather *who* we are building. We have a deep responsibility to treat those under us and those around us with extreme dignity and not as a means to an end. I'm reminded of two scriptures from the mouth of Jesus that are truly golden rules for living and leading and I'll close this chapter by imploring you to keep these in front of you always:

And as you wish that others would do to you, do so to them. (Luke 6:31, ESV)

Give, and it will be given to you. Good measure, pressed down, shaken together, running over, will be put into your lap. For with the measure you use it will be measured back to you. (Luke 6:38, ESV)

CHAPTER 13

THE LOST ART OF HONOR

> "No person was ever honored for what he received. Honor has been the reward for what he gave."
> -Calvin Coolidge

During the Renaissance period, Michelangelo painted the famous Sistine Chapel ceiling from 1508-1512. He moved from east to west, meticulously crafting one of the most iconic pieces of art in the history of the world. While we may not see works quite like Michelangelo's paintings being developed today, art in and of itself isn't necessarily dying; we see creative art and architecture all around us.

There are other lost art forms that seemingly don't exist anymore, though. For instance, you have to look really hard to find any sort of chivalry in today's society. You know what that is, right? It was a code of conduct that men (particularly knights) carried that encompassed high moral standards, a strong emphasis on honor, respect, bravery, and a selfless approach to treating women, children, and peers.[34] Today we may say it's chivalrous for

---

34. "Chivalry," Dictionary.com. www.dictionary.com/browse/chivalry.

a guy to hold a door open for a woman, but it goes much further than that. Chivalry at its core is about honor, and after these definitions, you will see how chivalry is a lost art.

I kind of like that definition of chivalry and I hope to assume those character traits, but it seems complicated and convoluted today. If you think I'm exaggerating, you haven't been to a tee-ball game in my neighborhood. You also probably haven't been watching your social media feed and you certainly didn't watch the past few local and national elections. Maybe you chalk all that up to theatre and don't take it seriously, and maybe you're right. Maybe. I've also listened to pastors gossip about other pastors and have heard "Christian" folks curse their leaders, churches, and pastors they don't even know. Where's the honor? I thought we were supposed to be on the same team, but we act like we're rivals or enemies. Honor seems to be on its deathbed and it'll take all of us to revive it.

So why does honor matter and how do we implement it back into society and relationships today? Let's find out.

What are some basic examples of honor still breathing in society? How about sumo wrestlers stomping their feet before they wrestle (a sign of respect), boxers touching gloves, soldiers saluting, athletes shaking hands after a game, standing ovations, and moments of silence. Those are good examples, right? Sure, on some level. But what is the real heartbeat of honor?

Honor is choosing to give respect even when you are disrespected. Honor is choosing to show decency when others have done nothing to deserve it. Honor is giving your enemies a place at the table, even if that means you have to stand. Honor is knowing when to be silent, even when you have the right answer and the leader does not. Honor is doing the hard thing that may slow your immediate progress or plans for the sake of trusting God's instituted leader. Finally, honor is submitting yourself and staying faithful to a leader, and remaining teachable when corrected. In fact, that's not just honor; that is *intelligence* as well. This, my friends, really is the Jesus way, and I'm not sure anything quite positions you for God's blessings like honor can.

THE PAYOFF

We are a multi-site church, meaning we are one church that meets in different neighborhoods. Finding a venue for our multiple congregations has been the hardest aspect of launching new communities, but *nothing* was more stressful than finding a venue and neighborhood to launch The Block's first location. When Lauren and I moved to Philly in November 2013, we knew we would need to attend and learn from a church in the neighborhood where we lived. So we attended, developed a relationship with the pastor, and got involved on their team for several months before we launched our church.

As I mentioned before, finding a place to have church was very complicated, and the compounding challenges of church in the city made finding a venue incredibly difficult. It had been months and months of searching and I felt under the gun, as I was running out of time to come under contract so that we could launch in the fall of 2014. A couple of months before our deadline, the only options that we had were venues in pretty close proximity to the church we were involved with. Even still, since we are in the city, over 100,000 people might live within a very small radius. However, the pastor of that church asked me early on not to plant our *first* church in "his" neighborhood, and while I didn't particularly want to agree to that, it didn't seem like such a big deal with so much of a runway to launch our church. With the pressure of my runway ending and only nearby venues opening to me, I was getting frustrated with this arrangement. I went back to him and said something like, "There are a lot of people between us, so I don't think it will be that big of a deal. I've had feelers out from people and venues all over the city and the only people who are getting back to me with opportunities are nearby. Would you please reconsider?" I could tell he was frustrated with me and I knew I had a choice to make.

It was a simple choice and a complicated one at the same time: do the hard thing and keep looking, or take the easy way out and launch nearby. During my prayer time, I'm confident I heard the Lord clearly say, "If you honor him, I'll bless you." "That's it, God? Can You at least tell me where to plant or what venue is available?" Nah—that's not really how the Lord tends to work. We often have to take faith leaps before those risks materialize into actual steps on a ladder toward Kingdom success. Pretty soon after I honored this pastor by keeping my word, God came through. We found a venue and still meet in that building today. In fact, we've launched two locations out of it, have helped resource other pastors and our city, and have planted churches around the world. Not only that, but on our two-year anniversary, we launched our second location almost exactly where I wanted to be when I first asked this pastor. His original request was that we not start our *first* church in that neighborhood, and they since had moved. Therefore, the door opened for location number two near where this church had been, and God has blessed that location as well. I specifically remember praying before we launched that second location; God spoke to me and said, "Do you remember when I asked you to honor that pastor? I haven't forgotten about it, even if you have. I'm going to bless this." He has, more than we could have imagined or asked for. His way is always the best way. (That pastor and I are still friends to this day and we've been a mutual benefit to one another. I'm glad we chose relationship over rivalry.)

BIBLICAL CONTEXT FOR HONOR

I hope that my story stirs a passion within you to make honor a priority in your life. I also want to give you a strong biblical precedent for this lost art in hopes that we can resurrect this element of God's plan into our culture.

In 1 Samuel 18:7, we see a young David returning from the battlefield to an exuberant Hebrew crowd chanting, "Saul [the current king of Israel] has slain his thousands, but David his ten thousands!" King Saul was insulted by this scene, and we see him engage in a pursuit to rid David from his kingdom. Saul's insecurities drove him mad and led him to lose his most valuable asset in David, but this particular chapter isn't as much about Saul's wrongdoing as it is about David's response and right doing:

> After Saul returned from fighting the Philistines, he was told that David had gone into the wilderness of En-gedi. So Saul

chose 3,000 elite troops from all Israel and went to search for David and his men near the rocks of the wild goats. At the place where the road passes some sheepfolds, Saul went into a cave to relieve himself. But as it happened, David and his men were hiding farther back in that very cave! "Now's your opportunity!" David's men whispered to him. "Today the Lord is telling you, 'I will certainly put your enemy into your power, to do with as you wish.'" So David crept forward and cut off a piece of the hem of Saul's robe. (1 Samuel 24:1-4, NLT)

As I read this passage, I see a few obvious action steps that David took as he embodied the principle of honor toward his leader. We can learn a thing or two from him about honor, so let's take a look:

IGNORE THE PEANUT GALLERY

As we see in verse 4, David's men reminded him that this was the day he had looked for and of which God had spoken to him when he was anointed to be king of Israel long ago. This moment would in fact put a period to his troubles and open the way to his advancement as king. At this point, Saul lay completely at David's mercy, and it was easy to imagine how little he had reason to show him. Even David's squad is saying, "Get him! End this!" Without looking deeper, we can quickly misunderstand the promises and processes of God.

Remember, God had assured David that he would deliver him from Saul, and his men interpreted this as a warrant to destroy

Saul. However, *God's promises never contradict God's principles.*
God wouldn't have us get ahead of Him, because He knows that
speeding past His timeline only leads to pain and setbacks later on. In fact, James talks about endurance in chapter one, verse
three of his book: "For you know that when your faith is tested,
your *endurance* has a chance to grow" (NLT). Endurance in this
context doesn't actually mean being able to run ten miles. No,
the original word, *hupo-monen*, actually means to stay under and
behind. In other words, don't take things into your own hands
and get ahead of God. Trust what He's spoken and don't contradict His character. For David, that meant shutting out the peanut
gallery and leaning into the only voice that matters, the voice of
God, our blesser.

May I remind you, just because it's for your benefit doesn't
mean it will be *for your benefit.* Culture will always tell you to take
advantage of your opportunities, whereas God's voice will tell you
to wait on Him. People may tell you to backstab, lie, cheat, hurt
someone else to get ahead, or make your boss look bad, but the
voice of God says something different. David understood God's
heart, and I'll prove it again. He writes:

> Be still in the presence of the LORD, and wait patiently for
> him to act. Don't worry about evil people who prosper or
> fret about their wicked schemes. (Psalm 37:7, NLT)

I want to tread lightly on this subject matter, but if you look at
recent riots in our nation, some of that was endorsed and ignited
by hate speech and encouragement from the peanut gallery. Is it
ever effective to destroy or kill leaders, police, or others because

you feel as if something is owed to you? *Never!* Wait on the Lord to be your defense and victor while proactively acting out God's character. Is it wrong to voice your hurt or struggles? No! Is it wrong to advocate for the least of these? No! Is it wrong to rally others to peacefully fight for what must change? No! Yet, the Word says:

> Dear friends, never take revenge. Leave that to the righteous anger of God. For the Scriptures say, "I will take revenge; I will pay them back," says the LORD. (Romans 12:19, NLT)

We must be vigilant and know when to shut off the noise of the peanut gallery and listen to the voice of God. Remember though, if you don't spend any time with God, you'll end up mistaking the voices of good-intentioned people for the voice of God.

LISTEN TO THE VOICE OF REASON

In verse 5, we see David's conscience begin to bother him because he had cut Saul's robe. Although David did no real harm to Saul, even though it was in his power to do so, he still wished he had not done it because it was dishonoring to Saul's authority and royal dignity. It is a good thing to experience conviction for sins that seem little; it is a sign that the conscience is awake and tender and will be the means of preventing greater sins later on. God is always speaking through His Spirit. Take a moment and listen; He will always provide a way out of sin. Passion is good, but at times it can lead us to do something wrong. Before we show *passion*, we might need to *pause*.

The temptations in your life are no different from what others experience. And God is faithful. He will not allow the temptation to be more than you can stand. When you are tempted, he will show you a way out so that you can endure. (1 Corinthians 10:13, NLT)

So, when you want to argue, show up late, disrespect, gossip, or retaliate, remember to *respond*; don't *react*. We respond when we listen to the voice of reason, and we react when we listen to the crowd. Our voice of reason comes from above.

MAKE UNPOPULAR DECISIONS

In verses 6 and 7, we read,

He said to his men, "The Lord forbid that I should do this to my lord the king. I shouldn't attack the Lord's anointed one, for the Lord himself has chosen him." So David restrained his men and did not let them kill Saul. (1 Samuel 24:6-7, NLT)

Not only would David not harm Saul by his own hand, but also he wouldn't let his men touch him either. Matthew Henry said, "Thus did he render good for evil to him from whom he had received evil for good, and was here both a type of Christ, who saved his persecutors, and an example to all Christians not to be overcome of evil, but to overcome evil with good."[35]

35. Matthew Henry, *An Exposition of the Old and New Testament*, Vol. II, 1828.

Everyone must submit to governing authorities. For all authority comes from God, and those in positions of authority have been placed there by God. (Romans 13:1, NLT)

In some of your social circles, it's going to be unpopular for you to support an unpopular president, police officers, your church, or your faith. Honor does what's unpopular to experience what's naturally unattainable. Is it possible your dreams are on the other side of your willingness to honor? It's possible that God is bringing to mind some opportunities for you to honor those who are difficult. Did your boss come to mind? How about your pastor? Did the Holy Spirit prompt you to pray for a government official? Did He ask you to take a humbling step of faith and apologize to someone? I have a feeling that you might be sensing that an uncomfortable step of faith is on the horizon. Don't hesitate; your best is on the other side!

RESPECT THE POSITION

We read in verses 8 through 11,

David came out and shouted after him, "My lord the king!" And when Saul looked around, David bowed low before him. Then he shouted to Saul, "Why do you listen to the people who say I am trying to harm you? This very day you can see with your own eyes it isn't true. For the Lord placed you at my mercy back there in the cave. Some of my men told me to kill you, but I spared you. For I said, 'I will never harm the king—he is the Lord's anointed one.' Look, my father, at what I have in my hand. It is a piece of the hem of your robe! I cut it off, but I didn't kill you. This proves that I am not trying to harm you and that I have not sinned against you, even though you have been hunting for me to kill me." (1 Samuel 24:8-11, NLT)

David treated Saul with the utmost respect, even humbling himself to bow low before him in honor. This example teaches us to treat all superiors, even those who we disagree with or who have hurt us, with the honor that is due them. Let me be very clear: *just because you honor the position, that doesn't mean you affirm their opinions or actions.* The Bible says to honor your mother and father (see Ephesians 6:1-3), honor your spiritual authority (see Hebrews 13:17), honor your governing authority (see Romans 13:7), and honor your boss (see Colossians 3:22). Be careful to not speak harshly about those who lead you, as easy as that can sometimes be. There is a way to ask for advice about how to deal with difficult leaders without cursing them or gossiping about them to others. You've already read quite a few examples of what honor truly is, but there might be something specific that God drops in your heart to do to honor your leader, including apologize. If I were you, I would pause right here and listen for that sweet voice of the Holy Spirit prompting you to make a move to please God and position yourself for a greater tomorrow.

As I close this chapter, I want you to remember that revenge and justice belong to God and God alone (see Romans 12:19). We can pursue it, but we will never attain it quite like God can. Yet, if we pursue honor, God will raise us up in just the right moment. In 1 Chronicles 10:1-6, we read that Saul was under such political pressure and was so overcome by war that he killed himself. Verse 6 says it best: "So Saul and his three sons died there together, *bringing his dynasty to an end*" (NLT).

Wouldn't you rather God do it than you force it? I sure would, and I hope you're convinced that honor is the key to more than we can ever ask, dream, or imagine.

CHAPTER 14

LOYALS

"Loyalty runs on sacrifices, those that cannot make sacrifices cannot be loyal to anybody."
-Younus Algohar

When starting a church, you're basically looking for anyone who is breathing to help you. If it's your grandma and she can wave, make her a greeter. If it's your dog and he can watch kids, throw him into kids ministry. Okay, so I'm kidding, but the point I'm making is that basically anyone is a candidate to get involved. This is what makes church plants exciting, difficult, sometimes really weird, and a great opportunity for anybody to be used by God and offer their gifts to His church.

I love that. I love looking for hidden talent or developing people whom nobody else said yes to. I like to brush off the dust or dirt that others see and get to the gold I knew was there all along. I like being in the people business for this reason and I love seeing those whom no one ever thought would amount to much leading at a high level. It makes what I do very much worth it. To do this though, we have to see with our spiritual eyes, not with our natural eyes. I'm grateful that, when we do, we're usually quite surprised with what we see.

LONGING FOR LOYALTY

Several years ago, before we launched, I was introduced to a couple that had just graduated from Bible college and were basically sitting around doing nothing. When I say "nothing," I don't actually mean *nothing*, but their potential wasn't being tapped in any way, shape, or form. Jeff was attending and serving at his dad's church that had never modernized. The philosophy of the church hadn't evolved with time, there weren't many young people, and there wasn't a vision for the future. Sharon, his brand-new (and very talented) wife, wasn't leading worship on the weekends or connecting relationally either. Both of them were frustrated and concerned that this was not the best fit for their new life together and that they weren't being utilized the way they knew God had called them. Sharon could tell she was drifting from her calling to lead people in worship and was becoming increasingly saddened by the circumstance she wasn't able to make a difference in.

At this point, both started to pray and wonder if there should be a next step for their marriage and ministry. Just about that time, I came calling. I got a tip from a missionary friend who had visited their church and was wondering why Sharon was sitting on the sidelines. I immediately called Sharon and invited them to consider joining our journey. Thinking back on all this, it's funny to me that Jeff and Sharon are the quintessential introverts and my rowdy, aggressive nature didn't allow Sharon to tell me that for the first several months I called her "Shannon" instead of her real name. She never corrected me, and we laugh about it to this day.

Let's fast forward a little bit. I had so many conversations with people as we were starting this church that I had forgotten that

Sharon and Jeff had a musical background, and they actually never reminded me. For months, they had been driving each week from way outside the city just to connect with us and possibly use their gifts in our church. See, what I loved and still love about them is that they were never about what they could do but more about what they could add. They didn't transition from their original church because they weren't being used properly; they transitioned because they had no place to serve, connect relationally, and be loyal to a mission. When we were trying out musicians at our launch team meetings, they were up third or fourth. When they got up to lead us, the presence of God rushed into the room and I fell to my knees and wept. I heard God say, "I've got this. Rest." It was a beautiful and sacred moment for me and I won't soon forget it.

Several years later, these two unassuming introverts from the sticks of Pennsylvania and Maine have played a prominent role in the day-to-day operations as well as every big moment our church has experienced. They are servants through and through and are defined by their loyalty to our mission. I could not be more grateful, because this is the example and precedent I want set for all of our ministries and people in our faith family.

Why did I tell that story? I want to use this as a springboard to talk about relationships with our church, our leaders, and our bosses. First, I need you to know that transitioning out of a church should be a last resort. There are so many people who leave churches when they were supposed to stay. Too often, the scenario is that we simply don't like how things are done or are offended for a myriad of reasons, so we leave before we can ever level up and help the church grow from the situation. To be honest, defining what constitutes leaving a church is complicated and there are so many factors that it could be a book in and of itself. The point I'm making is that leaving a church should only happen after much prayer, godly counsel, and attempts to make the place better. I also don't want to advocate staying in an abusive ministry or to sit under a heretical teacher. What I do want to address is the constant shifting and transitioning in our churches and in our lives. I want to address the lack of loyalty to a mission greater than ourselves.

OLD-SCHOOL

My grandfather, whom I call "Pop-pop," grew up in a time when you worked at one place for many years, then you got a pension and retired. You were loyal. I realize it is a different time now, but I also believe more of us can be more loyal. According to a survey, 43 percent of Millennials plan to quit their current job within two years. Only 28 percent plan to stay in their current role for more than five years. The survey is based on the views of 10,455 Millennials and 1,844 members of Generation Z questioned across 36 countries.[36] Some blamed the business ethics (or lack thereof) of their bosses and companies. Additionally, the lack of inclusion and diversity within the workplace rubs Millennials and Gen Zs the wrong way. Finally, these individuals want to leave because they feel unequipped to do their jobs at the highest level. The systems for necessary training and development aren't

36. Zack Friedman, "43% of Millennials Plan to Quit Their Job Within 2 Years," Forbes Magazine, May 22, 2018. www.forbes.com/sites/zackfriedman/2018/05/22/millennials-quit-job/#565950b757f1.

in place, and they desire to grow but sense they are unprepared for what could or should be next.

The article goes on to give seven different ways that employers can elicit loyalty from their young workers. I won't get into all seven because that's not what this chapter is about, but one of the points made was really compelling to me. It was actually idea number one in the article: *Younger workers want to understand what loyalty means from their employer's perspective.* This struck me because I believe that, internally, there's a desire in all of us to be loyal and experience loyalty.

If this is the first point mentioned, it must mean that people want to be loyal but are afraid of the consequences if they are. Will they be abused? Will they miss another opportunity? Will they make less money? The list goes on and on. I completely recommend doing all you can to protect yourself from abuse, and you should definitely do your homework when searching for a church or job. Please continue to "trust but verify" with your leaders. Yet, while these questions are valid and necessary, I often wonder if we put too much power in our own preferences and miss the blessings of God while attempting to attain our own treasure.

IT PAYS TO BE LOYAL

The story of Ruth and Naomi is a fascinating look at biblical loyalty, and I know it will remind us of a few necessary lessons we may have forgotten along the way. In the story, Naomi, her husband, and her two sons journey to a place called Moab to find food because of a famine, and they end up staying there to live. Her sons marry two Moabite women, one of them named Ruth.

Sadly, both of Naomi's sons and her husband die, but she continues to live with her daughters-in-law. Naomi eventually hears that the Lord helped the people of Israel and food has been provided back home, so she decides to move back to Bethlehem and tells Orpah and Ruth to stay in Moab and find new husbands.

While Orpah returns to her mother's home, Ruth responds differently:

> But Ruth replied, "Don't ask me to leave you and turn back. Wherever you go, I will go; wherever you live, I will live. Your people will be my people, and your God will be my God." (Ruth 1:16, NLT)

Upon returning to Bethlehem, Ruth has to normalize her life and get a job. In a roundabout way, Naomi plays matchmaker and hooks her up with a distinguished and well-to-do guy named Boaz. What attracts Boaz to Ruth is her loyalty to Naomi. This shows him that she can be trusted with more. Boaz and Ruth marry and have a son named Obed, who eventually has a son named Jesse, who becomes the father of King David, from whose genealogy comes the Savior of the world, Jesus. Yikes!

Ultimately, Ruth's loyalty led to legacy, and you can't buy that kind of favor. You can't predict or demand the benefits of your loyalty either. You can only know in your heart that God's Word never comes back empty (see Isaiah 55:11). You can now see why loyalty matters: it benefits you as much as it benefits the person to whom you are loyal. What strikes me the most about this story is that Ruth had no clue that going with Naomi would result in a new husband, a great life, and a rich heritage—not to mention that her story would go on to be told for generations. One difficult decision can point you toward significance, which is why trusting God's principles makes all the difference in your life. The idea of loyalty comes from God and He repeats Himself over and over again. I love what Deuteronomy 7:9 says: "know that Yahweh your God is God, the faithful God who keeps His gracious covenant loyalty for a thousand generations with those who love Him and keep His commandments" (HCSB). I also favor 2 Timothy 2:13: "If we are unfaithful, he remains faithful, for he cannot deny who he is" (NLT). Loyalty is who God is, and He rewards those who carry His character, especially when it is difficult to do so.

I WANT IT NOW

It's no secret that we live in a fast-food culture. This has been evolving since the growth of companies like McDonald's and the technological boom of the 1950s. I don't think it's a stretch to say that we are obsessed with how many "likes" we get on Instagram and are guilty of checking our phone minute by minute to see who's into us. While the rise of social media has created a beautifully connected culture, it also perpetuates an "I want it now" state of being.

What is it that we want now? I'm glad you asked. Usually, we want everything, even things that we know can be detrimental to our lives. "But everyone else has it!" It's human nature to think like this. Don't feel too bad. Think about it though: we want to be married when we're single. We want to be the boss when we're a first-year intern. We want to be celebrated when we should celebrate others. We want our own ministry but we haven't helped build anyone else's. We want a new job but we haven't been faithful with our current one. We want a raise but we've been working at the job for less than a year. We want a new leader but we haven't given this one a chance to lead. On and on it goes. *While it isn't wrong to want more for our lives, we often forget to want what's currently in our lives.* That's true happiness, remember? Wanting what you *have*. We gotta chill. Happiness usually occurs when we steward the relationships we've been given well, both the difficult and the easy ones. That's why loyalty, similar to honor, is complicated, because people aren't perfect. Yet, we please God with our loyalty and gain invaluable opportunities when we serve the people God has placed in authority over our lives.

LIVING MY BEST LIFE

My mom has been with her company for over thirty years. She's worked for the same guy for all of them and I've asked her many times why she never jumped ship when things were difficult. Her answer is always the same. Here's the main idea: "Joey, the man has given me a good life and lots of flexibility. He took a chance on me when I was young and I helped him build his company. I never was able to get a degree, and that didn't matter to him. I was a part of something bigger than myself. I've always had what I wanted because I wanted what I was given. It took some time but I made good money. I've owned multiple houses, you've gotten to attend more sporting events than you could have dreamed, and we've had the best life we could have asked for. We were sent to Florida and that's where we met Jesus. Before we came to Florida, I had another opportunity but decided instead to stay with my boss. Aren't you glad I did? I'm saying, it pays to be loyal! I would have done it all over again, even the really painful and challenging moments. Trust me, there were plenty." This always encourages me, especially because I'm a Millennial and my natural tendency is to look online for greener pastures or see everyone else "living better" than me on Instagram. However, I'm a firm believer in the old adage that life really can be greener where I water the grass. I can honestly say that for the most part, my mom lived her best life, and with God's help she way outreached her potential.

As I observed my mom's life, she organically taught me a few things about loyalty that I'd like to pass on to you. Hopefully these statements will infiltrate your relationships with the leaders in your home, work, and ministry. Take a look:

Prepare to be inconvenienced. If you're serving a leader, a company, or an organization well, you will be inconvenienced often. It's impossible for this not to happen if the mission is compelling and worthwhile, because anything or anyone with a great vision will lead you toward sacrifice.

Right after high school, I interned for my pastor and quickly learned the power of inconvenience. On day one of my internship, there was a hurricane where we lived and I spent my first week putting his fence back together. Initially, as an eighteen-year-old, I thought I was there to learn preaching, but I was there to learn something much more important in ministry: loyalty. After I overcame my initial frustrations, I spent the next three years waiting by the phone for an inconvenient call to pick something up, take his kids to an event, or help fix an issue with his car. You name it, I did it. Looking back, I'm so very grateful for those experiences because the best conversations, illustrations, and leadership lessons came from them. They also set me up to reap loyal relationships in my ministry today. I now have several young men who have functioned in that same capacity for me, and as I write this, I realize I couldn't do what I do without them. Their participation in my life and ministry is a direct result of my loyalty to my original pastor. *Every inconvenient moment was a seed sown that would sprout at the exact time I needed it to.* I highly encourage you to find comfort in being inconvenienced so that when it happens, it won't throw you for a loop. Inconvenience is truly for your good.

Play the long game. We have to stop thinking "me, me, me." The long game is about maturity and recognizing that future opportunities are predicated on how we manage our current ones. People are always our assignments, and serving those individuals and teams well is pleasing to God (which is the goal, of course). If you desire to have your own company or ministry, you must start now. The long game is the very best way to stay loyal and plan for your dreams at the same time.

So what is the long game and how do you play it? Well, a preacher friend of mine gave this illustration about waiting tables. He said that the best way to be loyal and not get caught up in worry about the future is to "serve while you wait." If a server is waiting on tables and it's a busy night, they may not know exactly when they'll be cut. I've noticed at times that a waiter can sense when his time is almost up and start to check out mentally. My drink isn't being refilled, the hot sauce is forgotten, our chips haven't been replenished, etc. However, the most effective table attendants are the ones who keep their heads down and don't worry about when their time is up. They also usually receive the biggest tips and that tends to make it worth it.

Point is, play the long game. According to Psalms, your steps are ordered (see Psalm 37:23). God hasn't forgotten about your dreams, goals, or hopes. In the meantime, keep your head down, keep working on your gifts and talents, keep developing strategic relationships, and let God handle your next stop.

Focus on the mission. When you find yourself frustrated with a leader or employer, remember why you took the role or submitted yourself to their leadership in the first place. Hopefully, the mission was compelling and you believed in it. When you're disappointed, focus on the mission. When you're angry, focus on the mission. When they are unclear, focus on the mission. Before you quit, ask yourself if there is anything more you can do to fulfill the mission of this company or organization. Sometimes the beauty of the mission reinvigorates us and stabilizes our emotions long enough to respectfully figure out our next steps.

Guard your words and attitude. What you do should reflect what you say. If one does not reflect what they say in what they do, they are deceiving themselves. James 1:26 says, "If you claim to be religious but don't control your tongue, you are fooling yourself, and your religion is worthless" (NLT). There are real consequences both emotionally and to your future when you speak harshly or in a disloyal way about those who lead you. Paul says in Corinthians that we have authority to destroy arguments of the enemy and take every evil thought captive. This happens when we guard our tongues and the culture of our language. Your words have the potential to cause extreme stress and perpetuate anger, bitterness, and envy in your life and the lives of others. I promise, if you speak evil about your leader now, you're asking for it later. Now, you absolutely should bring issues to your leader (we talked about this in a previous chapter), but spreading venom around has a price tag. Be careful.

Transition well. The art of transitioning is one of the most misguided and convoluted activities in my generation. In fact, the church in general hasn't been great at this either and we must fix it. Transitions will happen, and sometimes they need to. How we go about them makes all the difference. Personally, I don't think that we transition well for two reasons: (1) we don't know how and weren't instructed properly, and (2) we don't value loyalty. I've seen so many bad transitions in my life and I simply cannot stand watching them. We need to do better and it boils down to loyalty, respect, honor, and integrity. The choice is ours. Choose well.

I love the picture of Elijah (the legendary prophet) introducing Elisha (future prophet) to his ministry in 1 Kings 19. It's radical and absurd. Elijah throws his cloak on Elisha and walks away, almost as if he's being obedient to God by developing a mentee but not making it easy on anyone to follow him. Some leaders really are afraid of developing others because they're insecure and want all the glory. They are loyal to themselves alone. I don't think this was Elijah's heart. In the story, Elisha proceeds to chase after him and says something like, "Let me say goodbye to my family." And Elijah is pretty much like, "Nah, brah. Now or never! This is basically going to be horrible, so you better know what you're getting into!" Elisha was all in though. He went back and destroyed everything that represented his old life and career. He knew that Elijah wasn't playing around, and if he was going to get everything out of this mentorship program, he had to give *all* he had as there was no room for a Plan B.

> When the Lord was about to take Elijah up to heaven in a whirlwind, Elijah and Elisha were traveling from Gilgal. And Elijah said to Elisha, "Stay here, for the Lord has told me to go to Bethel." But Elisha replied, "As surely as the Lord lives and you yourself live, I will never leave you!" So they went down together to Bethel. (2 Kings 1:1-2, NLT)

I love this passion from Elisha. Sensing that his time with Elijah was ending, he stayed loyal to the very end. Elijah tried to sneak away two more times, but Elisha refused to let him go without him. Other colleagues tried telling Elisha that this was the day Elijah was leaving, but Elisha hushed them. He loved his leader so much. Their relationship was beautiful, and the benefits of Elisha's loyalty are next level.

Now, before I go on about the glories of his loyalty, I need to highlight why transitioning well is important for both parties.

Elijah trained Elisha for multiple chapters. He showed him the ropes, the good and the bad. In 2 Kings 2:9, the Bible says,

> When they came to the other side, Elijah said to Elisha, "Tell me what I can do for you before I am taken away." And Elisha replied, "Please let me inherit a double share of your spirit and become your successor." (NLT)

Elijah was prepared to give him more than he had. That's the Kingdom. That's loyalty. That's our call. When we transition away from a place or a person, there are a few important things that should happen that we see riddled throughout this story:

1. Show them all you can show them or learn all you can learn.
2. Leave them better than you found them.
3. Prepare for the coming transition. Both parties should have an idea that something different is near.
4. Equip them to do better without you.
5. Impart your DNA, your value system, and your mission into your mentee or employee. If you're the mentee, receive these things, embrace the position, and appreciate how they got to where they are.

The Bible shows us that Elisha performed twice as many miracles as Elijah. Many theologians and commentators allude to the fact that Elijah was similar to John the Baptist, as one who would prepare the way. Elisha is seen as a gracious and humble type of Christ who performed ministry with extraordinary compassion. We can interpret for ourselves that Elisha was greater. So, for our purposes, loyalty surely pays.

CLOSING THOUGHTS AND QUESTIONS

It is both my hope and my prayer that because of this book, you have acquired a fresh perspective and passion for healthy relationships. I didn't set out to answer all the questions about sex, dating, marriage, friendships, and church. I did, however, aim to spur you on to pursue health personally, emotionally, and with those you know and don't know yet. We need each other, and I've proven that we are biblically called to be in community with one another. Quality relationships are the currency of life and they last for generations. Sadly, so do the consequences of failed relationships. If you want to expand your network, sustain lifelong friendships, and ultimately make the most fulfilling life for yourself, getting better at relationships is an essential step. If you believe this book has helped you level up, please let me know and spread the word on any and all platforms. I believe your best can be *now* and that it is definitely *ahead*!

Here are a few questions I hope you ponder and answer as our time together ends:

1. Are there things about you that need to be addressed that are inhibiting quality relationships? If so, what are they and how can you get some help with them (e.g., counseling, conversation, etc.)?

2. Are there relationships in your life that need repair that you've been avoiding?

3. Is there anyone you need to forgive?

4. Is there a faith community you've avoided getting involved with out of fear?

5. Do you need to move on from some relationships that are hurting your emotional health and journey with God?